Data Products Volume 2: Data Product Management Platform

Scaling Data Products

AF871069

Paolo Platter

Technics Publication
SEDONA, ARIZONA

TECHNICS PUBLICATIONS

115 Linda Vista, Sedona, AZ 86336 USA

https://www.TechnicsPub.com

Edited by Steve Hoberman

Cover design by Lorena Molinari

All rights reserved. No part of this book may be reproduced or transmitted in any form or by any means, electronic or mechanical, including photocopying, recording, or by any information storage and retrieval system, without written permission from the publisher, except for brief quotations in a review.

The authors and publisher have taken care in the preparation of this book, but make no expressed or implied warranty of any kind and assume no responsibility for errors or omissions. No liability is assumed for incidental or consequential damages in connection with or arising out of the use of the information or programs contained herein.
All trade and product names are trademarks, registered trademarks, or service marks of their respective companies and are the property of their respective holders and should be treated as such.

WIthout In any way limiting the author's exclusive rights under copyright, any use of this publication to "train" generative artificial intelligence (AI) technologies to generate text is expressly prohibited. The author reserves all rights to license uses of this work for generative AI training and the development of machine learning language models.

First Printing 2026

Copyright © 2026 by Paolo Platter

ISBN, print ed.	9798898161200
ISBN, Kindle ed.	9798898161217
ISBN, PDF ed.	9798898161224

Library of Congress Control Number: 2026932868

This book is dedicated to the people who made this journey possible long before it had a name.

First, to my wife Alice and my family.
Being an entrepreneur is not simply a profession. It is a state of mind that rarely switches off. You do not clock out at the end of the day, and you rarely lift your foot completely off the accelerator. Even when you are physically present, part of your mind is still somewhere else—solving a problem, anticipating a risk, thinking about the next decision that could change everything.
Her understanding of what that truly means is what made this entire path sustainable. She understood that there are seasons when intensity is not optional, when presence looks different, when building something from scratch requires a level of commitment that is difficult to explain from the outside. That understanding was never loud, never theatrical—but it was constant. And without it, none of this would exist.

To my children, Edoardo and Francesco.
One day, you will understand why some evenings were longer, why sometimes I was thinking about something you could not see. I hope that what remains is an example of commitment. Not the company we built, but the mindset behind it: the courage to start something uncertain, the resilience to continue when things are difficult, and the responsibility to finish what you begin. If you inherit anything from this journey, I hope it is that.

And to my parents, Franca and Mauro.
Long before I ever called myself an entrepreneur, they had already shaped that instinct in me. They transmitted something much deeper than ambition: the habit of taking responsibility, the reflex to build rather than complain, the idea that risk is not something to avoid but something to approach with intelligence, integrity, and hard work. Whatever I have created rests on foundations they built quietly over decades.

This book is also dedicated to my co-founder, Alberto Firpo.
We started with little more than belief—two people, two laptops, and an idea that could easily have failed. Over fifteen years, we grew from just the two of us to a company of more than 300 people. And in all that

time, there was not a single real fracture between us. No destructive arguments. No ego battles. No moments where trust was in question.
It was, in many ways, a match made in heaven.
Entrepreneurship tests people. It exposes weaknesses, magnifies pressure, and forces difficult decisions. Through all of that, we operated with absolute trust in each other's capabilities—not blind trust, but earned trust.

Alberto created the conditions for me to grow as a professional. He trusted me with complex situations. Many of the lessons behind these pages were forged in those moments.
Scaling a company is difficult.
Scaling trust over fifteen years is even harder.
We managed to do both.

Finally, this book belongs to all the Agilers—the people with whom I grew professionally.

Through endless debates, disagreements, architectural battles, and late-night production incidents, we sharpened each other. Those honest conversations shaped how I think about platforms, governance, autonomy, and systems. The ideas in this book were not born in isolation; they were shaped in confrontation, refined in practice, and tested in reality.

If this book has any depth, it is because of those years of shared obsession with doing things properly.
On the surface, these pages speak about data products, governance, and platforms.

But underneath, they are about trust, responsibility, resilience, discipline, and love—the invisible architecture behind everything that lasts.

If this book helps organizations decentralize responsibly, create value sustainably, and build systems that empower people rather than constrain them, then it is also a reflection of that support.
Let us begin.

Endorsements

Decentralisation without structure always looks like freedom at first and chaos soon after. Paolo Platter's great contribution is showing, in concrete and hard-won detail, that the self-service platform is what keeps that boomerang from coming back. This is not a book of frameworks or slogans; it is a hard-earned account, built on years in the room where these decisions actually get made, of how autonomy and governance reinforce each other when the platform is designed correctly. Anyone leading a data or platform organisation should read it before the next reorganisation, not after.

Bjørn Broum, Data Strategist and Enterprise Architect, writing on data strategy and organisational learning at *My Field Notes*

Paolo Platter possesses a rare combination of profound technical expertise and genuine open-mindedness. In a landscape where data management is rapidly evolving, his innovative approach to decentralization is exactly what the industry needs. Paolo is a remarkable listener who is never afraid to explore uncharted paths and challenge the status quo. I have the utmost personal and professional respect for him; he is a true pioneer, capable of driving a paradigm shift and changing how we manage data on a global scale.

Pierpaolo Ruggiero, Data Platform Manager, Hera Group

I had the challenge to build a data platform from scratch, now used by an incredibly high number of developers in my company. Paolo Platter contributed to that success with his deep experience not only in data management, but also on how people and organizations work together. The decentralized approach is a delicate balance between technology and human factors, and Paolo has a unique ability to navigate both.

Over the years I've crossed paths with Paolo repeatedly, at conferences, tech events, and in direct work collaboration, and every time I've come away with the same impression: a genuine drive for innovation paired with a real willingness to learn and share with the community.

Any book carrying a year of his work and experience deserves serious attention from anyone building modern data platforms.

Marco Santoni, Head of Data and Analytics Platform

When it comes to making decentral data management work Paolo is a genuine visionary and a dedicated builder. What strikes me most is his indepth expertise in dealing with data product management challenges from a system design perspective, providing enterprises with elaborate answers.

Jan Stiebing, CDO Deutsche Börse Group

I have been impressed by Paolo's ability to combine strategic thinking with practical execution. Throughout our interactions, he has consistently demonstrated deep expertise in modern data management, platform thinking, and decentralization. What I particularly value is his ability to help transform ambitious visions into concrete and actionable approaches.

Paolo has not only helped us make our own vision more tangible and pragmatic, but has also provided valuable insights into market developments, validating where the industry is heading and what is required to stay ahead. His combination of thought leadership, practical experience, and collaborative mindset makes him a trusted advisor and a highly respected professional in the data management community.

Paolo is passionate about helping organizations move from theory to results, creating value by bringing together people, processes, and technology.

It has been a pleasure to exchange ideas with Paolo, and I look forward to seeing his insights and experience shared through this book.

Wouter van Straten
Data Management Architect at KPN in The Netherlands

Contents

Introduction

In recent years, many organizations have embraced the idea that data is not just an asset—it is a product. A product with a purpose, a lifecycle, an owner, and a consumer. This shift represents more than a semantic adjustment. It changes how we design, build, govern, and evolve the systems that generate and distribute value from data. It forces us to move beyond publishing datasets and toward deliberately engineering Data Products with the same discipline we apply to software products.

In the first volume of this series, *Data Product Management: The Core Concepts*, we explored the foundations. We examined what a Data Product is, how to define its lifecycle, clarify ownership, and measure value. That book addressed the "what" and the "why".

This book focuses on the "how".

More precisely, it focuses on the enabling platform—the self-service data platform—which stands as one of the four pillars of Data Mesh. In my view, it is the structural pillar that keeps the other three upright. Volume 1 established three central findings. First, a data product is not defined by its presence in a catalog, but by the boundary of accountability it establishes—the convergence of responsibility, authority, and lifecycle control within a clearly defined perimeter. Second, ownership is meaningful only when it extends to the production chain: assigning names to datasets without granting authority over how they are produced, validated, and evolved creates the appearance of ownership without its substance. Third, federated governance needs more than organizational intent. Without a mechanism to enforce shared standards computationally—not through documentation and social pressure alone—federating data management at scale produces inconsistency rather than autonomy.

Volume 2 begins where Volume 1 ends. If you accept those three findings, the next question is unavoidable: What infrastructure must exist to make that model operational at scale?

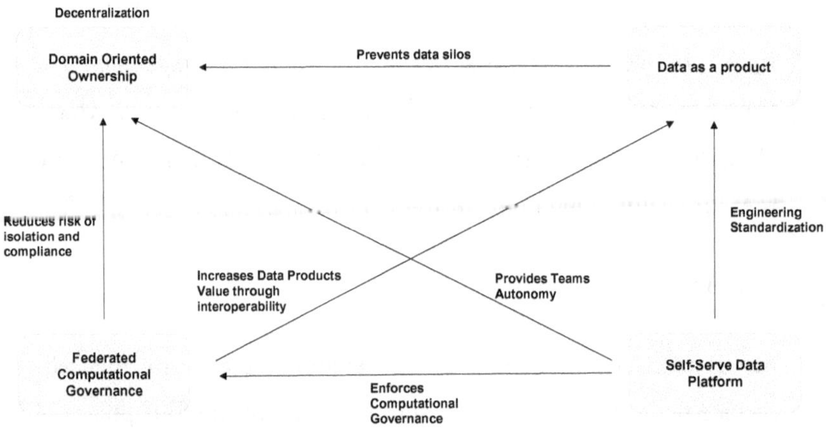

Data Mesh rests on four interconnected principles:

- Domain-oriented ownership.
- Data as a product.
- Federated computational governance.
- Self-service data platform.

These principles do not live in isolation. They reinforce each other. Domain ownership without engineering standardization leads to fragmentation. Data as a product without governance leads to chaos. Federated governance without automation becomes bureaucracy.

The self-service platform connects them. It provides the engineering standardization that makes Data Products interoperable. It enables teams with autonomy while ensuring computational governance at deploy time and runtime. It prevents silos not by centralizing ownership, but by standardizing how Data Products are built, described, deployed, and evolved.

Without the platform, decentralization becomes wishful thinking. With the wrong platform, decentralization becomes an uncontrolled explosion.

We will explore this relationship step by step. I will not anticipate every conclusion here. Instead, throughout this book, we will gradually uncover why the platform is not just an enabler but the structural backbone that makes the entire model viable.

I did not arrive at this conviction through theory alone.

In late 2019, during one of the first large-scale Data Mesh initiatives at the third-largest utility company in the world, I was tasked with designing the architecture for the platform that would standardize and govern the creation and change management of Data Products. It was a complex, multi-country, multi-business enterprise. The scale was intimidating.

For the first time in my career, we did not begin with discussions about performance, scalability, or specific technologies. We started with a different question: How do we standardize the way people build and evolve Data Products so that, regardless of who creates them or when, they remain interoperable, discoverable, and governed by design?

I had previously built frameworks that attempted to guide development through documentation, best practices, and architectural principles. They looked solid on paper. Over time, however, they created tight coupling between the platform team and domain teams. They slowed down innovation. They generated frustration. Eventually, they eroded trust.

In large enterprises, especially those operating across countries and business units, guidelines alone do not hold. Complexity stretches them until they break. Informal agreements decay. Architectural purity erodes under delivery pressure.

I realized that if we truly want decentralization—if we genuinely believe that domains should own their Data Products—then we cannot rely on voluntary alignment. We need an enabling platform that embeds standards into the engineering process itself. We need automation that makes the right path the easiest path.

The platform becomes indispensable in any serious decentralization initiative. So indispensable that it deserves an entire book.

I believe deeply in the decentralization of data management and AI practices. I believe organizations can unlock extraordinary value by distributing ownership to the domains that understand the business context best. But decentralization without structure turns into a boomerang. It creates duplication, inconsistency, and compliance risks. It fragments the landscape and ultimately pushes organizations back towards centralization.

This book exists to prevent that boomerang effect.

We will explore how to design a self-service platform that accelerates time to market while increasing governance automation. A platform that supports autonomy without becoming a gatekeeper. A platform that does not prescribe one architecture forever, but that remains resilient as technologies and organizational structures evolve.

We will examine how computational policies, standardized templates, lifecycle management, and embedded governance transform abstract principles into operational reality. We will discuss not only technical components, but also the social dynamics that determine whether a platform empowers teams or constrains them.

Because at its core, this topic is not only technical. It is socio-technical. It sits at the intersection of engineering, organizational design, incentives, and trust.

This book is for platform engineers and architects designing internal platforms that must scale across domains. It is for Data

Product managers and domain leads who struggle to balance autonomy with standardization. It is for governance teams who want to move beyond checklists and manual approvals towards computational enforcement. It is for executives and transformation leaders searching for a realistic path to decentralized data with reasonable investment and sustainable time to market.

Whether you are building your first data product management platform or evolving an existing one, this book aims to help you avoid common traps and build something that lasts.

ONE

The Data Management Problems We Keep Ignoring

This first part of the book is deliberately uncomfortable.

Not because the ideas are complex, or because the technology is hard, but because the failure modes we are about to explore are painfully familiar. Most organizations struggling with data products and decentralization in general are not blocked by tooling. They are blocked by the way they work, the expectations they set, and the shortcuts they accept along the way.

By the time technology becomes "the problem", the damage is usually already done.

This part brings together five patterns that quietly undermine data product initiatives before they ever have a chance to scale—patterns that are visible in retrospect but rarely named in real time.

The first is tool bias: the belief that adopting a new platform, catalog, or orchestration engine will fix what is fundamentally a structural and cultural problem. It does not. Tools amplify whatever practices already exist in the organization, for better or worse.

The second is the Data Product trap: the habit of calling existing datasets "data products" without establishing the ownership, authority, and lifecycle control that make the label meaningful. The result is inflated expectations and eroded trust.

The third is the decentralization illusion: granting autonomy to domain teams without providing the shared structure—contracts, guardrails, lifecycle conventions—that makes distributed ownership sustainable rather than entropic.

The fourth is the governance-after-the-fact problem: treating compliance as an inspection activity that happens after deployment, rather than as a property designed in from the start.

The fifth is the internal platform trap: treating a platform as a one-off project rather than a long-term product commitment—and paying the price when adoption stalls, usability degrades, and teams quietly route around it.

The goal of this chapter is not to blame tools, teams, or methodologies. It is to make these structural issues visible—because you cannot design a solution to a problem you have not yet named clearly.

Tools are Not the Problem

Most data initiatives fail when organizations mistake tool sophistication for the harder work of ownership, process, and accountability. The story always starts with genuine ambition. Leaders want faster insights, better decisions, and more autonomy for teams. They invest in modern platforms, hire specialists, adopt new architectures, and proudly announce that data is now a "product".

Expectations rise quickly. Reality, however, moves at a very different pace. When progress stalls, the reaction is almost always the same. The warehouse is too slow. The catalog is incomplete. Pipelines are fragile. The platform is not mature enough.

A new tool is procured, or a new framework is introduced, with the hope that this time the problem will finally disappear. What rarely gets questioned is the underlying assumption: that better technology can compensate for unclear ownership and goals, fragmented processes, misaligned incentives, and poor understanding of the business context.

In most organizations, data initiatives inherit decades of habits. Data is treated as a side effect of systems, not as something deliberately engineered. Responsibilities are blurred. Teams optimize locally, often heroically, but without a shared definition of what "done" actually means. Governance appears late, as an audit or a checklist, disconnected from how data is produced and evolves day to day. In this context, no tech tool can succeed.

Technology does not fix broken ways of working. It amplifies them. If the underlying practices are weak, new tools will only help you fail faster and at greater scale. The way an organization works with data matters far more than the tools it uses. Software engineering makes the point plainly. Switching from Java to Python, or from C++ to Java, does not magically improve the quality or robustness of the software produced inside an organization. Without skilled engineers and a solid engineering process (versioning, testing, reviews, clear ownership, and accountability), the quality of the output remains exactly the same. Only the syntax changes. The same logic applies to data.

Without teams that understand what they are building, why they are building it, and who they are building it for, no platform will save the initiative.

A data product built without ownership, quality discipline, and lifecycle thinking will remain fragile, regardless of whether it runs on the latest cloud stack or the most fashionable architecture. The analogy extends well beyond IT. Imagine a car factory. You can change the materials, replace the robots, or buy more advanced assembly tools. But if the production process is not oriented toward total quality, if defects are not detected early, if responsibility is unclear, if feedback loops are weak, the final car will not be better. It may even be worse, because the factory now produces defects faster and more efficiently.

Tools are not useless. Far from it. They are extremely good at specific things:

- They help reduce waste.
- They lower operational costs.
- They improve efficiency and repeatability.
- They automate steps that humans should not have to perform manually.

Tools create efficiency. Quality requires something different entirely.

Quality comes from the attention people put into what they build, and from the mechanisms in place to protect that quality over time. These mechanisms are foundational:

- Clear ownership, so someone is accountable for the outcome.
- Reviews, so mistakes are caught early.
- Quality checks and guardrails so behavior matches expectations.
- Explicit responsibilities, so work does not fall through the cracks.
- Incentives aligned with long-term value, not short-term delivery.

When attention inevitably drops because people are under pressure, deadlines approach, or priorities shift, these mechanisms allow the organization to notice the degradation and correct course before consumers are affected. A platform can help enforce these mechanisms, but it cannot invent them. If the organization has not agreed on how data products are built, owned, and evolved, automation will simply encode confusion into software.

If your organization does not share a clear way of working for data products (how they are designed, validated, released, operated, and changed), no amount of technology will compensate for that gap. New platforms will only make the cracks more visible. They will expose inconsistencies, surface ownership conflicts, and highlight governance weaknesses that were already there.

Data initiatives stay stuck in that loop for exactly this reason: the organization keeps treating technology as the lever, when the real leverage sits in practices, responsibilities, and incentives. Until those foundations are addressed, tools will continue to disappoint. They are being asked to solve problems that only ownership, discipline, and shared ways of working can address.

The Data Product Trap

As soon as the idea of data products enters an organization, a subtle but recurring trap tends to emerge.

The expression itself spreads rapidly. It appears in strategic presentations, internal communications, transformation roadmaps, and architectural guidelines. What previously had different names is gradually reclassified. Over time, almost everything that moves data begins to be described as a data product. The language evolves at a remarkable speed, and that linguistic shift can create the reassuring perception that something equally substantial is happening beneath the surface.

In practice, the change often begins at the narrative level rather than the structural level.

Existing datasets are reframed within a new vocabulary. They are described more carefully, documented more thoroughly, and positioned more intentionally inside a marketplace. A point of responsibility is assigned, making the asset easier to discover and explain. From the outside, this layering of clarity and visibility makes the transformation appear real. Yet the mechanics that generate, transform, and govern the data frequently remain untouched. The upstream systems are the same. The production logic is the same. The change management process, if it existed at all, remains unchanged.

When "data product" becomes interchangeable with "well-presented dataset," the organization risks confusing packaging with progress. In some cases, this confusion can be more damaging than inertia, because it creates the illusion that a structural shift has already occurred. The organization believes it has embraced product thinking, while the operational foundations required to sustain that mindset are still missing.

Catalogs and marketplaces are not new inventions. For years, organizations have documented assets and made them searchable. Renaming an artifact and placing it in a marketplace does not, by itself, alter how it is produced, how it evolves, or why it should be trusted. What it does alter are expectations. The word "product" carries implicit promises: stability, managed evolution, accountability, and responsiveness to consumer needs. When real structural capabilities do not back those promises, the gap between perception and reality widens.

At the center of the gap between perception and reality lies the concept of ownership.

Ownership, in a product sense, means full accountability for a product's existence, behavior, and evolution—not a contact to call when something breaks. True ownership implies responsibility for bringing something into existence and for ensuring that it remains valuable over time. It requires the authority to influence how the data is generated, transformed, validated, and changed. It includes the power to deliberately manage breaking changes, prioritize improvements, and adapt the asset to evolving functional requirements, quality expectations, and regulatory constraints.

Without that authority, the term "owner" becomes largely symbolic.

In many organizations, individuals are assigned ownership of datasets that they do not truly control. They may not have visibility into upstream modifications. They may not be able to alter the transformation logic that shapes the data. They may lack the mandate to enforce backward compatibility or to invest in structural quality improvements. When consumers report issues, these so-called owners often find themselves mediating between teams rather than steering the product directly. Responsibility exists, but the levers of change sit elsewhere. This situation creates an imbalance that is difficult to sustain.

Accountability without control gradually turns into liability.

Consider a straightforward example: a CSV file exported from an operational system. Suppose that file is now documented in detail. Its fields are explained, its business meaning clarified, and a responsible person is formally associated with it. The file appears in a marketplace alongside other assets labeled as data products. From a consumer's perspective, it may look indistinguishable from something more mature.

Yet structurally, it remains what it was. There may be no formal contract governing its schema. No process may exist to detect and manage breaking changes. If the upstream application changes the file format, downstream consumers may only discover the change when their processes fail. If a column's meaning shifts over time, the impact may be felt silently across reports and models before anyone traces it back to its source. If data quality deteriorates, the designated owner may have no direct authority to intervene in the originating system.

Enhanced documentation does not resolve these vulnerabilities. Nor does assigning ownership, if that ownership does not extend to the production chain.

In fact, applying the label "data product" to such an artifact can accelerate disappointment. Consumers interpret the label as a signal of managed evolution and reliability. When reality falls short of that expectation, trust erodes more rapidly than it did when the asset was simply known as a dataset.

A genuine data product is not defined by its visibility in a marketplace or by the elegance of its description. It is defined by the boundary of responsibility it establishes.

That boundary encompasses more than the data itself. It includes the logic that produces and transforms it, the metadata that formalizes its meaning, the policies that constrain its acceptable use, and the lifecycle mechanisms that govern its evolution. Together, these elements form an operational unit that can be intentionally steered. Without them, the artifact remains dependent on external forces it cannot control.

When a team truly owns a data product, it owns the full chain from input to output. It can respond to consumer feedback not merely by documenting limitations, but by adjusting implementation. If new attributes are required, if quality standards must be raised, or if compliance requirements change, the team has both the mandate and the capability to act. Evolution becomes deliberate rather than accidental.

Absent that ability to steer, the substance of product thinking is missing, even if the terminology is present.

When organizations overlook this distinction, tensions emerge quickly. Delivery teams are encouraged to publish data products but are not given the structural authority required to manage them end to end. Governance functions begin to expect guarantees that the underlying architecture cannot consistently enforce. Consumers encounter assets that look mature yet behave unpredictably.

The result is a gradual erosion of confidence. Consumers feel that promises are not being met. Producers feel burdened by expectations that exceed their actual control. Governance teams sense a widening gap between declared standards and operational reality.

Over time, what was introduced as a progressive shift toward modern data management risks being dismissed as another fashionable concept that failed to deliver. The disappointment, however, does not stem from the idea of data products themselves. It stems from a structural mismatch between the label and the capability behind it.

If ownership is limited to documentation, if production logic remains outside the product boundary, and if change management cannot be enforced coherently, then calling something a data product does not merely stretch the definition. It distorts incentives, inflates expectations, and undermines trust.

A data product is not created by renaming an artifact.

It emerges when responsibility, authority, and lifecycle control converge within a clearly defined boundary—and when that boundary is respected over time.

The Decentralization Illusion

Decentralization is frequently presented as the natural remedy for slow, centralized data organizations. The narrative is persuasive: when a central data team becomes a bottleneck, the obvious solution is to distribute responsibility across business domains. Give teams autonomy, and speed will follow. Delivery will accelerate and Ownership will become clearer, boosting Innovation.

There is substance in this argument. Without Autonomy, teams struggle to respond to evolving business needs, external dependencies constantly reshuffle priorities, and accountability becomes diluted across layers of coordination. When every decision must pass through a central authority, delivery slows, motivation declines, and ownership becomes symbolic rather than real. In that sense, decentralization addresses a genuine structural tension.

The difficulty arises when autonomy is treated as an end state rather than as a condition that must be engineered carefully. Autonomy, on its own, does not scale; it fragments.

When each domain is free to define what a data product is, how it should be implemented, how it should be described, and how it should evolve, local optimization begins to dominate. Teams make reasonable decisions within their own context. They choose patterns that fit their skills, constraints, and immediate goals. Over time, however, these locally sensible choices start to diverge. Interfaces evolve in slightly different directions. Naming conventions reflect domain-specific habits. Quality thresholds vary subtly but significantly. Duplication creeps in quietly, until it becomes increasingly difficult to determine which product is authoritative and which is an approximation.

In such a landscape, interoperability is no longer designed deliberately. It becomes something that occasionally happens, almost by accident.

In the early stages, decentralization often feels energizing. Teams move quickly within their boundaries. They no longer wait for central approvals or architectural sign-offs. They experience a renewed sense of control. Yet the moment a use case spans multiple domains, the friction becomes visible. Integrations require negotiation rather than composition. Dependencies are managed through ad hoc agreements rather than shared conventions. Changes ripple unpredictably, and their impact is difficult to anticipate.

A paradox gradually emerges: individual teams may feel faster, but the organization as a whole becomes slower.

Governance, in this context, shifts into a reactive stance. Without common patterns and shared expectations, it can only intervene after issues materialize. Data quality problems are detected downstream. Security weaknesses are discovered late in the lifecycle. Compliance concerns are addressed retrospectively, often under pressure.

> *Governance becomes associated with obstruction rather than enablement, not because its intent is misaligned, but because it lacks the structural levers to act earlier.*

This is where many decentralization initiatives begin to stall. The challenge is not that autonomy was misguided; it is that autonomy was introduced without an accompanying framework capable of sustaining it. Execution was decentralized, but intent was not standardized.

The pattern is not unique to data.

In software engineering, allowing each team to choose its own language, framework, deployment model, and coding standards can initially accelerate delivery. Over time, however, the organization accumulates a mosaic of services that are difficult to operate consistently. Onboarding new engineers becomes increasingly complex. Cross-team collaboration requires translation layers. Operational overhead grows. Eventually, more effort is spent on integrating and maintaining than building new capabilities.

Manufacturing offers a similar lesson. If each plant defines its own production processes, quality controls, and component specifications, local efficiency might improve in isolation. Yet as soon as components must be assembled across facilities or serviced in different regions, incompatibilities surface. Parts do not align. Quality varies. Costs rise. The absence of shared standards undermines the scale the organization intended to achieve.

Urban development tells the same story. Cities that expand rapidly without shared rules for infrastructure, zoning, or safety may appear dynamic in the short term. Over time, congestion, inefficiency, and inequality become entrenched.

Retrofitting coherence into a system that has grown without coordination proves far more expensive than embedding it from the beginning.

Across these domains, a consistent lesson appears: freedom without coordination does not create sustainable speed. It increases entropy.

Data ecosystems are not exempt from this principle. Structure is often perceived as the opposite of agility, yet in practice, it is the condition that allows agility to persist over time.

A shared lifecycle establishes a common cadence for designing, validating, releasing, and evolving data products. Guardrails clarify what must remain consistent across the organization while preserving room for domain-specific optimization where it truly adds value. Explicit ownership boundaries prevent accountability from dissolving as complexity increases.

Such a structure does not suppress autonomy; it makes it viable.

When shared expectations are clearly articulated and embedded into the operating model, teams can act independently without renegotiating foundational assumptions at every integration point. Consumers benefit from predictable behavior and managed evolution. Governance can move upstream, becoming a proactive enabler rather than a downstream auditor. Change becomes tractable because its scope and impact are bounded.

Without these foundations, decentralization does not eliminate bottlenecks; it multiplies them. Instead of a single central constraint, the organization accumulates numerous local ones, each concealed behind different conventions, standards, and interpretations of what constitutes a data product.

Genuine decentralization is the deliberate design of a system in which teams can operate autonomously precisely because boundaries, responsibilities, and guardrails are clear.

Governance After the Fact Does Not Scale

In many organizations, governance is treated as something that happens *after* the work is done. Teams build first. Data is produced, pipelines are deployed, and datasets are published. Only later does governance step in to check whether everything is compliant, documented, and acceptable.

On a small scale, this model can appear to work. When there are only a handful of data products and a limited number of teams, manual reviews, periodic audits, and catalog-based assessments feel manageable. Issues are visible. Corrections are painful, but still contained.

The illusion breaks the moment adoption grows.

As soon as data products multiply and teams start moving in parallel, governance after the fact collapses under its own weight. Audits, catalogs, and manual controls always arrive too late. By the time a problem is identified, the data is already in use. Consumers have already integrated it. Dashboards, reports, and models already depend on it.

At that point, fixing the issue is no longer a simple correction. It requires coordination across teams, rework in multiple places, and sometimes breaking downstream consumers. The cost is not just technical. It is organizational.

A key misunderstanding sits at the heart of this model: confusing **assessment** with **governance**.

Governance after the fact is, at best, an assessment activity. It tells you whether something complies with a set of rules. It produces reports, findings, and recommendations. But it does not give you the ability to steer.

True governance means having the power to influence outcomes. It means shaping how data products are built, released, and evolved. It means being able to prevent certain behaviors, not just observe them once the damage is done.

When governance only assesses after deployment, it has no leverage. It can point out problems, but it cannot avoid them. It can raise flags, but it cannot stop bad data from propagating or architectural drift from accumulating. In practice, it becomes a spectator, commenting on decisions that have already been made.

Late governance interventions create predictable tension.

Delivery teams feel blocked. From their perspective, they have already delivered value, and governance is now asking them to go back and redo work under pressure. They see governance as a tax on delivery, something that slows them down without helping them succeed.

Governance teams, on the other hand, feel ignored. They are brought in too late, expected to "fix" issues they had no chance to influence. They are held accountable for risks without being given real control over how those risks are created.

Delivery teams learn to see governance as a hurdle to clear or bypass, not a partner to engage with. Governance teams respond by adding more checklists, more documentation requirements, and more manual reviews. The process becomes heavier, slower, and increasingly disconnected from reality.

Governance after the fact also creates a dangerous illusion of safety.

Catalogs look complete. Documentation is filled in. Checklists are ticked. Reports show high compliance scores. On paper, everything appears under control, while in practice, nothing fundamental has changed.

Bad data can still flow downstream before anyone notices. Breaking changes can still surprise consumers. Security and compliance gaps can still surface in production. Architectural inconsistencies continue to grow, quietly and cumulatively.

This is governance as theatre. It produces artifacts, not reliability. It measures symptoms, not causes. The organization feels governed, but behaves exactly as before.

Scalable governance cannot be reactive. It must be proactive.

That does not mean slowing teams down or centralizing decisions. It means embedding governance into the way data products are built and released. It means shaping behavior at build time, when decisions are still cheap and reversible, rather than policing outcomes after deployment.

Proactive governance provides guardrails between perception and reality instead of checkpoints.

It encodes standards into templates, pipelines, and automation. It makes the right thing easy to do and the wrong thing hard to do, allowing teams to move fast *within* clear boundaries.

Most importantly, preventative governance restores the true meaning of governing: the ability to steer. To influence direction and reduce risk before it materializes, aligning local autonomy with organizational goals.

An Internal Platform is a Product

Faced with these challenges, many organizations reach a familiar conclusion: *We should build our own platform.*

The reasoning feels solid. Data product management is not just a technical problem. It cuts across processes, organizational structures, incentives, and governance. It is deeply contextual. Who could possibly understand these nuances better than the organization itself? Buying a tool feels risky. Building feels safer, more controllable, and more aligned with internal realities.

And so, internal platform initiatives are born.

They almost always start with the best intentions and with strong technical teams. Existing CI/CD pipelines are extended to handle data workloads. Infrastructure-as-code is introduced to standardize provisioning. Templates are created to guide teams toward "approved" patterns. Piece by piece, a DIY data platform begins to take shape.

In the early stages, progress feels tangible. There is finally something concrete, where before there was only discussion. Teams can point to pipelines running, repositories being created, and automation kicking in. Compared to the previous chaos, this feels like a real step forward.

But over time, familiar problems begin to surface.

The platform is designed by engineers, for engineers. This is not malicious; it is simply a reflection of who is building it. As a result, non-technical contributors are excluded by default. Business stakeholders, governance experts, and product-oriented roles struggle to participate meaningfully. YAML files, scripts, and pipeline logs become the primary interface to the platform.

Meanwhile, complexity quietly accumulates. CI/CD workflows grow longer and more intertwined. Governance logic gets hardcoded into pipelines and scripts that are difficult to reason about and even harder to change. Each new requirement adds another condition, another exception, another workaround. Coupling increases, flexibility decreases.

The most important issue, however, is more subtle:

The platform is not treated as a product.

There is no clear vision for the user experience. No explicit definition of who the users are and what problems they are trying to solve. Adoption is assumed, not measured. Feedback is informal and reactive. Roadmaps are driven by urgent requests rather than by a coherent product strategy. The platform grows as a collection of capabilities, stitched together to address immediate needs, rather than as a cohesive system designed for long-term use.

The hidden costs appear gradually.

Time to market stretches as even small changes require careful coordination and testing. Maintenance starts absorbing more and more of the platform team's capacity. Keeping the existing system running becomes harder than adding new value. The platform team, initially meant to be an enabler, slowly turns into a bottleneck.

Eventually, domain teams adapt. They find shortcuts. They bypass parts of the platform. They build parallel solutions to move faster. The platform is no longer the default path; it is something to work around.

At that point, the organization has not built an enabler. It has built another system to manage.

The core misunderstanding is treating platform building as a one-off project. A platform is a long-term product commitment and it requires continuous investment in usability, evolution, and support. Ignoring this reality does not just slow things down. It becomes one of the most expensive mistakes an organization can make on its data journey.

Key Takeaway

- If you do not fix how people build data products, no tool will save you.
- Technology matters, but it is never the starting point. Ownership, lifecycle, governance, and structure come first. Without them, data products fail quietly, long before anyone blames the platform.
- In the next chapter of the book, we will shift focus. We will explore what it actually means to build a Data Product Management Platform that addresses these problems by design, rather than reacting to them after the fact.

Two

Data Product Management Platform

If chapter 1 was about dismantling a set of comforting illusions, this one is about rebuilding on much firmer ground.

By now, a pattern should be clearly visible. The failure of data product initiatives is rarely accidental, and it is almost never the result of a single bad decision. It follows recurring, predictable paths. Autonomy is introduced without the structure needed to sustain it. Governance is defined on paper but never truly executed. Platforms are approached as collections of tools, rather than as systems that shape behavior over time. Each of these choices can appear reasonable when taken in isolation. Combined, they quietly make scaling impossible.

In this chapter of the book, we deliberately change perspective.

Instead of asking which tool to buy next, or which framework to adopt, we step back and ask a more fundamental question: What kind of system is actually required to make data product management work in the long run? Not for a single enthusiastic team. Not for a controlled pilot. But for an organization that wants to grow, evolve, and adapt without constantly reinventing itself.

This chapter answers that question across six chapters. The first asks why a platform is not optional—why the tension between self-service and control cannot be resolved through guidelines or good intentions alone. The second defines what a Data Product Management Platform is and how it differs from the data tools that precede it. The third examines what it means to treat a platform as a product rather than a project—and why that distinction determines whether teams adopt it or route around it.

The remaining three chapters go deeper into the three properties that make a platform genuinely enabling: embedded automated governance (the shift from documents to executable rules), guardrails rather than golden cages (constraints that protect without prescribing), and the explicit balance between autonomy and governance (what the platform controls, and what it deliberately leaves free). This shift in focus is crucial. Tools matter, but only insofar as they support a coherent vision. What really determines success in decentralization is how ownership is enforced, how governance is embedded, how change is managed, and how teams are enabled to do the right thing by default, not by exception. The idea of an enabling platform emerges from this question.

A Data Product Management Platform is Not Optional

Many organizations still frame the platform discussion as a trade-off to be negotiated. On one side sits self-service: teams move fast, choose their tools, and own their outcomes. On the other side sits control: standards, security, compliance, and risk management. The underlying assumption is that strengthening one inevitably weakens the other.

This framing is wrong.

Self-service without control does not create freedom; it creates fragmentation. Teams optimize locally, interfaces drift, duplication grows, and interoperability becomes accidental. Over time, the organization loses the ability to reason about its own data landscape and to understand how value is exchanged between producers and consumers.

Control without self-service does not create safety either. It creates bottlenecks. Central teams become overloaded, delivery slows down, and decisions are taken far from the context in which data is produced and used. Autonomy disappears, teams disengage, and people start working around the system instead of with it.

The real challenge is not choosing between self-service and control, but designing a system that allows both to coexist and reinforce each other.

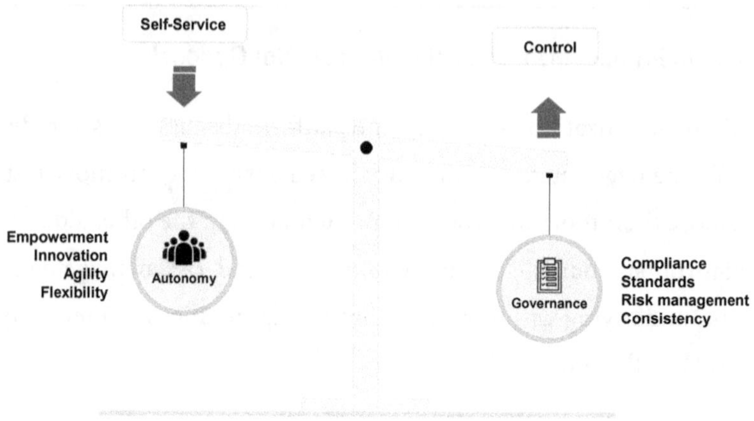

This is precisely the role of a **Data Product Management Platform**.

On the **agility** side, such a platform must enable value exchange between parties. Data products only make sense if producers and consumers can interact easily, with clear promises and predictable behavior. The platform must also foster genuine user autonomy and independence, enabling teams to move without constant central coordination. At the same time, it must reduce complexity by standardizing what should not be reinvented every time, so teams can focus on what actually differentiates their products.

On the **governance** side, the responsibilities are complementary rather than opposed. The platform must guarantee data governance and compliance by design, not through manual checks after the fact. It must protect each user from the misconduct or mistakes of others, ensuring that one team's shortcuts do not become another team's incident. And it must guarantee technical and data interoperability, so that decentralization does not result in a patchwork of incompatible solutions that cannot evolve together.

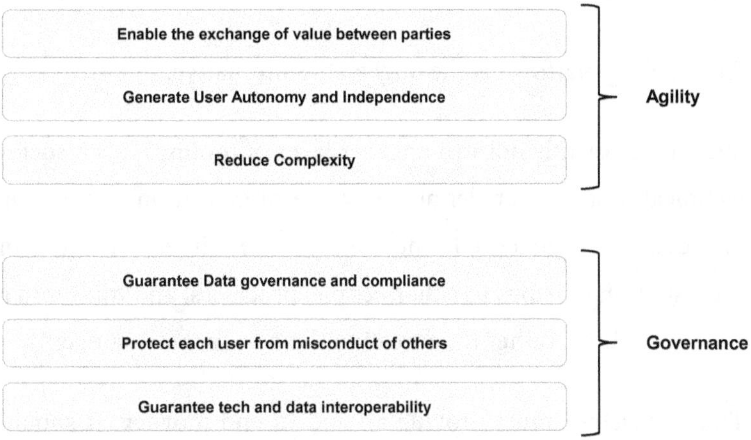

Without a platform, decentralization relies on trust, documentation, and good intentions. Teams are expected to do the right thing by reading guidelines, interpreting policies, and coordinating manually with other teams. This model can work when the organization is small, homogeneous, and informal. As soon as scale increases, regulation tightens, or people change roles, it breaks down.

Manual governance, human memory, and informal agreements do not scale.

Faced with this, some organizations swing to the opposite extreme and centralize everything into a single team or process. That may simplify coordination on paper, but it creates a different and equally damaging failure mode. Delivery slows down, local context is lost, ownership erodes, and innovation suffers. The organization becomes rigid precisely when it needs to remain adaptable.

An enabling platform is the only viable alternative.

Such a platform is not just another layer of tooling. It is a socio-technical system that defines how the organization wants data products built, governed, and evolved over time. It creates an ecosystem that brings together people, processes, and tools into a coherent whole, rather than treating them as separate concerns.

This **ecosystem** must provide an end-to-end journey. It should guide platform teams, data product teams, governance experts, and business contributors to do the right things, at the right moment in the data product lifecycle, with the right level of quality. It should reduce cognitive load, remove unnecessary friction, and make correct behavior the default rather than the exception.

Calling the platform socio-technical is not a theoretical nuance. The platform does not simply integrate technologies. It actively shapes behavior. Every default, every validation, and every automated check sends a signal about what matters and what does not. Over time, these signals influence how teams collaborate, how responsibilities are understood, and how decisions are made.

This is why a Data Product Management Platform is not optional. Without it, organizations are forced to live with permanent trade-offs between speed and safety, autonomy and trust. With it, those trade-offs become explicit design decisions, embedded into a system that allows the organization to scale, remain interoperable, and exchange value without losing control or momentum.

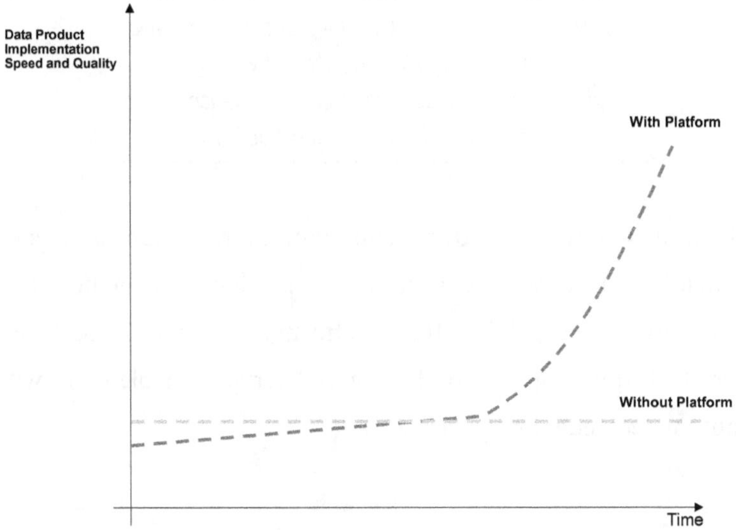

What is a Data Product Management Platform?

A Data Product Management Platform is a platform designed to enable the creation, ownership, and lifecycle management of data products in a **decentralized**, self-service way, while maximizing governance and minimizing cognitive load for teams.

Its purpose is not to replace the data platform or execution technologies, but to sit above them and define *how* data products are conceived, built, governed, and evolved over time. It provides the Control Plane for data products: a shared system of rules, abstractions, and automation that allows multiple teams to work independently without fragmenting the ecosystem.

A Data Product Management Platform makes ownership explicit, embeds governance throughout the lifecycle, enforces contracts and policies by design, and provides a guided, end-to-end experience for the roles involved in data product delivery.

Instead of relying on documentation, coordination, and good intentions, it turns decentralized data product management into an operational capability. It is a platform that operationalizes data product thinking by combining self-service enablement with automated, federated governance.

Who Needs a Data Product Management Platform?

A Data Product Management Platform is relevant for organizations that want to move towards decentralized data management without recreating silos, losing control, or duplicating effort and cost.

These are typically not organizations at the very beginning of their data journey. More often, they are companies that already have a solid data platform in place: data lakes or warehouses, ingestion pipelines, transformation tools, orchestration engines, and analytics capabilities. From a purely technical standpoint, they can already manage data end to end.

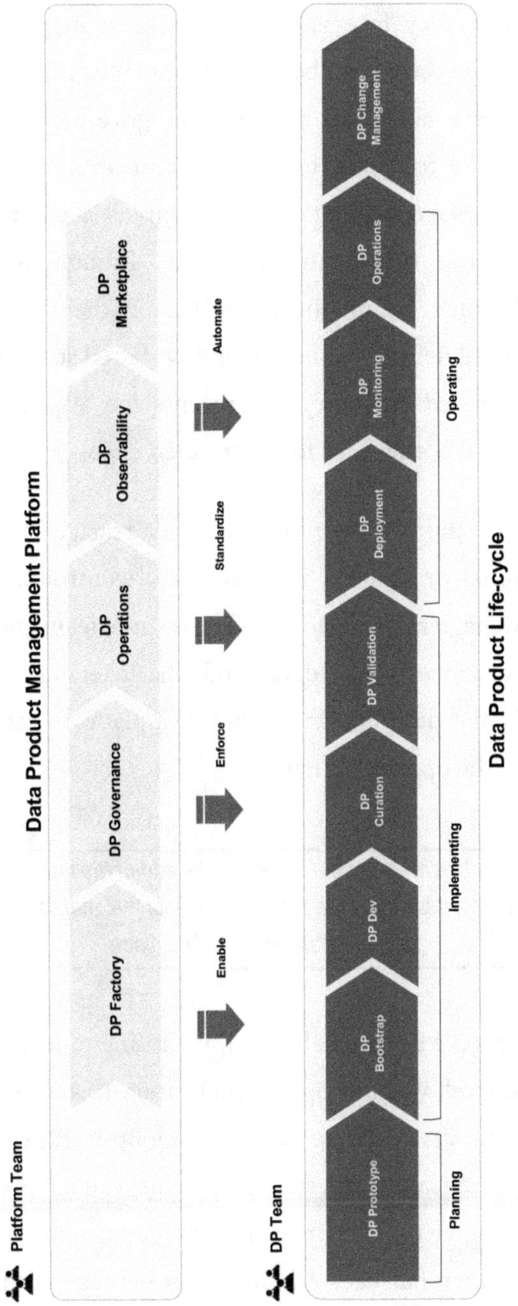
Platform Team
Data Product Management Platform
DP Factory
DP Governance
DP Operations
DP Observability
DP Marketplace
Enable
Enforce
Standardize
Automate
DP Team
DP Prototype
DP Bootstrap
DP Dev
DP Curation
DP Validation
DP Deployment
DP Monitoring
DP Operations
DP Change Management
Planning
Implementing
Operating
Data Product Life-cycle

The problem they face is not a lack of tools, but a lack of coherence. The ecosystem becomes fragmented across teams and domains. Data quality is uneven and governance is manual. Initiatives take too long to land because every new use case requires bespoke coordination. Autonomy exists, but it does not scale. For these organizations, a Data Product Management Platform becomes the missing layer. It allows them to decentralize ownership and delivery while preserving shared standards, shared trust, and shared efficiency. It prevents the organization from trading central bottlenecks for distributed chaos.

Many organizations believe they must first reach a certain level of organizational or cultural maturity before introducing a Data Product Management Platform. They assume teams need to fully understand concepts like data products, federated governance, ownership, and decentralization before a platform can be useful. In practice, the opposite is true.

The platform is not the reward at the end of the maturity journey; it is one of the main instruments that makes that journey possible in the first place.

Expecting people to internalize new operating models purely at a conceptual level, without operational support, is slow and error-prone. Without concrete feedback loops, experimentation remains theoretical, interpretations diverge, and confusion grows. Teams may agree on principles in workshops, but when it comes to delivery, they fall back to old habits because nothing in the system reinforces the new ones.

A Data Product Management Platform provides that reinforcement. It guides teams through new concepts by embedding them into daily work. It allows teams to *experience* decentralization, ownership, and federated governance through practice, without requiring them to master all the theory upfront. Learning happens through doing, not through abstraction.

The parallel with DevOps is instructive. No organization became "DevOps mature" before adopting tools like GitHub, GitLab, or CI/CD platforms. Those tools were not introduced after the methodology was fully understood; they were the means through which the methodology became tangible and repeatable. Without enabling platforms, DevOps maturity would have remained stuck at zero.

Data Product Management follows the same pattern. If an organization wants to move toward decentralized and federated data management, it must also provide the platform that makes this model operable. Maturity does not precede the platform, but it grows with it.

Platform as a Product

One of the most common and costly mistakes organizations make is treating the platform as a framework rather than as a product.

At first glance, the two may look similar. Frameworks come with structure, guidance, and reusable components. They promise flexibility and reuse. But their underlying logic is very different, and in a data product context, that difference matters enormously.

Frameworks are typically delivered and then quietly forgotten. They take the form of scripts, SDKs, reference implementations, and "best practices" that are handed over to teams with the expectation that they will adopt them, adapt them to their needs, and maintain them over time. Responsibility is implicit and fragmented. When something breaks, it is unclear who should fix it. When something needs to evolve, coordination becomes slow and painful because no one truly owns the whole.

Products behave differently because they assume responsibility by design. A platform treated as a product has a clear owner. It has users, not an abstract set of "stakeholders". It has a roadmap shaped by adoption, feedback, and outcomes, not just a backlog of incoming requests. It evolves deliberately, guided by what improves the experience and effectiveness of its users, not by what happens to be technically interesting to build next.

This distinction is not semantic. It determines whether the platform becomes a long-term enabler or a growing liability.

Frameworks assume that teams will assemble the pieces correctly and consistently. Products assume responsibility for delivering a working experience end to end. Frameworks push cognitive load onto users, forcing them to understand how everything fits together. Products absorb that cognitive load, hiding unnecessary complexity while preserving flexibility where it actually matters.

In the context of Data Product Management, this difference is decisive. Data product teams are already dealing with complex problems: business logic, data modeling, quality expectations, delivery pressure, and stakeholder demands. Asking them to also reason deeply about infrastructure, governance rules, security constraints, and lifecycle mechanics is unrealistic. Over time, it leads to frustration and disengagement.

A platform treated as a product does not remove complexity from the system; it contains it. It exposes services instead of artifacts. Teams interact with the platform itself as a service, so dedicated support, clear changes and releases, and backward compatibility are considered and respected.

As a result, trust starts to emerge.
Not because the platform is powerful or sophisticated,
but because it is predictable.

When the platform behaves consistently, teams stop looking for workarounds. When it evolves transparently, teams stop fearing change. When ownership is clear, responsibility becomes shared rather than contested, and collaboration replaces blame.

Frameworks tend to fail over time, while products endure. Frameworks ask users to adapt themselves to the system. Products adapt to users, while still protecting the coherence and integrity of the system as a whole.

Embedded Automated Governance

Governance is one of the most overloaded and misunderstood words in data management. It often evokes images of committees, documents, approval workflows, and long discussions. While these mechanisms may have worked in highly centralized environments, they simply do not scale in a decentralized data product ecosystem.

In a data product context, governance cannot limit itself to observation. It must execute.

Monitoring data quality after the fact does not prevent incidents; it merely reports them. Reviewing architectures once systems are already in production does not stop drift; it only documents it. Auditing compliance after release does not protect consumers; it explains, too late, why something went wrong. If governance cannot operate at the same speed as delivery, it gradually becomes irrelevant.

There is another important point that is often missed. In a Data Product Management Platform, we are not talking about *data governance alone*. We are talking about IT governance in the broadest sense. Governance must cover change management, architectural consistency, data behavior, security, privacy, and compliance as a single, coherent system. All of these dimensions together create the level of control that makes decentralization and team autonomy possible in the first place.

Data governance on its own is not enough. You can define quality rules, business terms, and ownership, but if teams are free to introduce breaking changes without control, adopt incompatible architectures, or automate infrastructure that bypasses security standards, the organization will still fragment. Decentralization does not fail because teams lack goodwill; it fails because the system does not provide enough protection against divergence.

For this reason, governance must be both embedded and automated. Embedded means that it lives inside the lifecycle of data products, not alongside it as a separate activity. Automated means that it executes as software, not as human interpretation.

Guidelines are suggestions. They rely on people reading, understanding, and applying them consistently under pressure. Policies, when expressed as executable rules, behave very differently. They become constraints that the system enforces automatically and consistently, across all governance dimensions: architectural rules, change management policies, security controls, and data guarantees.

When governance is implemented as computational policies, it becomes part of the platform's behavior. Descriptors are validated before deployment. Non-compliant releases are blocked by default. Breaking changes are explicitly detected and managed. Runtime guarantees are checked continuously. Evidence is produced as a natural by-product of execution, rather than being assembled manually when an audit arrives.

This shift fundamentally changes the relationship between delivery teams and governance functions. Governance is no longer perceived as an external authority passing judgment after the fact. Instead, it becomes an infrastructure service that protects everyone's autonomy. Teams can move faster precisely because the system absorbs complexity and enforces boundaries for them.

Teams receive fast feedback when issues are still cheap and easy to fix. Expectations are clear because they are enforced consistently, not negotiated repeatedly. Audits become simpler, because the evidence already exists and reflects what actually happened, not what was documented afterward.

Most importantly, governance stops being a negotiation. It becomes a shared contract between the organization and its teams, encoded directly into the platform that enables decentralization to work at scale.

Guardrails, Not Golden Cages

One of the most common fears when introducing platforms and automated governance is the risk of over-constraining teams. The concern is easy to understand. Nobody wants to end up in a golden cage: a beautifully designed system that looks elegant on paper but makes anything outside a predefined path either impossible or painfully expensive.

This fear is justified. Over-opinionated platforms do exist, and many of them fail precisely for this reason. They optimize for control so aggressively that they suffocate from the very autonomy they were meant to enable. Teams stop experimenting, creativity moves elsewhere, and the platform slowly becomes irrelevant.

The alternative, however, is not removing constraints altogether. That would simply reintroduce chaos. The real challenge is designing *better* constraints.

This is where the idea of guardrails becomes fundamental. Guardrails are not cages. They do not dictate every move or prescribe a single "correct" path. Instead, they define safe boundaries within which teams can operate with confidence.

Guardrails make the right thing easy and the wrong thing hard, without making exploration or innovation impossible.

In practice, this mindset translates into a very different set of design choices. Defaults instead of mandates. Templates instead of rigid, one-size-fits-all pipelines. Validation instead of outright prohibition. Visibility instead of micromanagement.

When a team wants to create or evolve a data product, the platform should naturally guide them towards compliant and interoperable choices. Not because they are forced to follow a narrow path, but because deviating from it requires conscious effort and explicit justification. The friction is intentional and proportional, not absolute. This approach respects autonomy while protecting the ecosystem as a whole. Teams retain the freedom to innovate, experiment, and adopt new patterns when they see fit. At the same time, they do so knowingly, with a clear understanding of the trade-offs and consequences for the wider organization.

There is also a deeper reason why golden cages are counterproductive. As Gregor Hohpe explains in Platform Strategy, innovation in a platform always happens at the edges. It emerges where users have room to express themselves, stretch the system, and occasionally push beyond its intended paths.

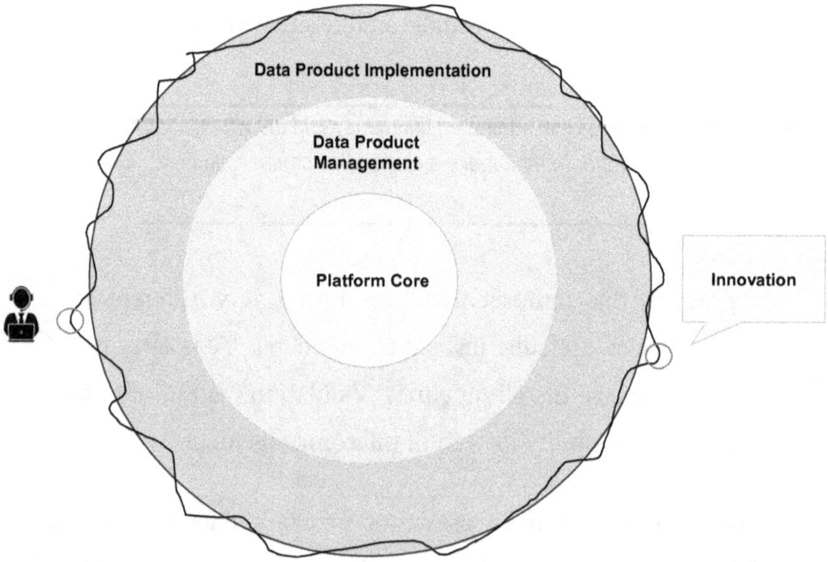

If that freedom of movement does not exist, the platform team loses its most valuable signal. They can no longer observe what users are trying to do outside the predefined flows. They cannot see emerging needs, creative workarounds, or new patterns taking shape. As a result, the platform cannot evolve in a direction that is genuinely useful to its users, because it is blind to their unmet needs.

Guardrails make this learning possible. By allowing controlled deviation, they expose where the platform is too rigid, where abstractions are missing, and where new capabilities should emerge. Golden cages, by contrast, hide these signals entirely.

In the end, the difference is subtle but critical. Golden cages optimize for control. Guardrails optimize for sustainability. One is built on the assumption that teams cannot be trusted, while the other assumes they can, as long as the system supports them in doing the right thing.

Autonomy vs Governance: Deciding What to Control

One of the hardest design decisions in a Data Product Management Platform is deciding where to leave freedom to teams and where to deliberately introduce control. This choice cannot be arbitrary, nor driven by personal preferences or organizational politics. The main driver for this choice should be global or common interest.

Not all platform capabilities have the same impact. Some choices affect only the internal efficiency of a single data product team. Others directly influence the health, sustainability, and scalability of the entire community of users and data products. These latter capabilities act on what we can call *global interests.*

Global interests are those areas where a shared approach generates disproportionately higher value for everyone. Semantic and data interoperability are a good example. If each team defines business concepts differently, the cost of integration explodes and reuse becomes accidental. Similarly, technical interoperability determines whether data products can be composed, replaced, or evolved without constant rework. Security and cost control also fall squarely into this category: one team's shortcuts can expose the entire organization to risk or generate uncontrolled spend that everyone else has to absorb.

Whenever a capability contributes to these global interests, it is worth intentionally increasing centralization, governance, and automation. In these areas, sacrificing a degree of individual freedom is not a limitation, but an investment. The value created at the ecosystem level far outweighs the local flexibility that is given up.

The opposite is also true. There are many areas where enforcing standardization provides little or no global benefit. Business logic is a clear example. Whether a data product team implements its transformations in Python or Java does not affect the wider ecosystem, as long as the data product behaves as expected from a consumer's perspective. What matters is not the internal implementation choice, but the external contract: schemas, semantics, quality guarantees, and behavior over time. Imposing control here would only slow teams down without improving interoperability or safety.

The same reasoning applies to many internal design decisions: how teams organize their code, how they structure internal pipelines, or how they optimize local performance. These choices should remain close to the teams, because they primarily affect local outcomes and innovation speed.

The role of the platform, then, is to deliberately draw this line. It should maximize user freedom where innovation is local and contained, and increase governance where choices have systemic consequences.

Automation and self-service become the mechanism that allows this balance:
by embedding governance into the platform,
teams gain freedom to operate safely within boundaries that protect the global interest.

Seen through this lens, autonomy and governance are not opposing forces. They are complementary levers. Governance protects what must remain coherent at scale. Autonomy fuels innovation where diversity is an asset rather than a risk. A well-designed Data Product Management Platform makes this distinction explicit and operational, allowing both to coexist without friction.

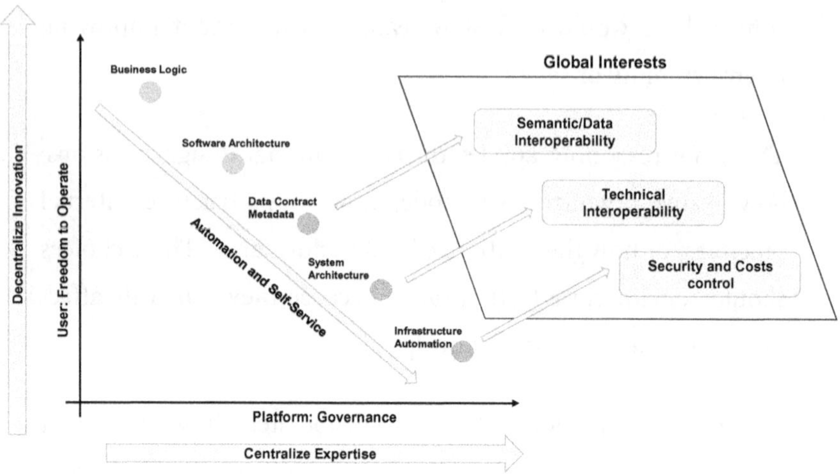

Key Takeaway

- The platform does not restrict autonomy it makes autonomy sustainable.
- By shifting from tools to systems, from rules to guardrails, organizations stop fighting the same battles over and over again. They encode their intent into software. They reduce cognitive load. They create an environment where teams can move fast without breaking trust.

In the next chapter of the book, we will move from principles to structure. We will explore how such a platform is designed, how its core components fit together, and how to avoid the architectural traps that quietly undermine even the best intentions.

THREE

From Principles to Platform Architecture

Chapter 1 named the failure modes. The second argued that only a platform—designed as a product, governed by embedded automation, and constrained by guardrails rather than golden cages—can prevent those failures at scale. Now the question changes. Not "What should the platform do?" but "How should the platform be built?"

This chapter translates intent into structure. It starts with architecture principles: not abstract ideals, but concrete design decisions that determine whether a platform can evolve, whether governance can scale, and whether data products can be trusted over time. These principles—evolvability, non-over-definition, separation of control and data planes, embedded governance, and contracts-first design—are the constraints that every subsequent architectural choice must satisfy.

From those principles, the logical architecture emerges. The logical model defines what the platform must be capable of, independent of technology: lifecycle management, governance, factory, operations, observability, cross-cutting capabilities, and the integration layer that binds them. Each capability solves a distinct class of problems; each boundary prevents a distinct class of coupling.

The physical architecture then answers the implementation question. Microservices as the natural realization of bounded contexts. Technology agnosticism as a non-negotiable constraint. Composability as the property that allows the platform to grow without accumulating debt. Integration-first as the pattern that keeps the Control Plane honest and the data plane free.

Finally, the platform metamodel and data product metamodel establish how the platform reasons about what it manages—the formal vocabulary that makes governance computational and evolution safe.

This chapter of the book is dense with structural reasoning. Readers who want to build, evaluate, or evolve a Data Product Management Platform will find the decisions here foundational—not as a blueprint to copy, but as a framework for making the trade-offs visible and the reasoning explicit.

Architecture Principles

Designing for a future we cannot predict

Too many data platforms fail because they start with architecture and end with disappointment. Boxes get drawn, tools get selected, and technologies get locked in. Only later does the organization realize that the system cannot evolve, cannot absorb change, and cannot survive the next paradigm shift. At that point, the architecture is already too rigid to adapt, and the platform becomes part of the problem it was meant to solve.

In this chapter of the book, we reverse the order.

Before building an enabling platform, we need to be clear about what must remain true even when everything else changes. Technologies will evolve. Organizational models will shift. Use cases we cannot imagine today will become critical tomorrow. The only real defense against this uncertainty is a set of principles strong enough to guide decisions long after the original architecture becomes obsolete.

Every successful architecture and every sustainable platform is built on principles, not on tools, patterns, or technologies, because principles endure. They provide direction when requirements are unclear, and they offer consistency when the system grows beyond what any single team can fully comprehend.

Without principles, architecture becomes reactive.

Decisions are made case by case, driven by short-term needs, individual preferences, or local optimizations. At first, this can look like flexibility and agility, and exceptions and workarounds are easy to justify. But over time, the cost accumulates and the fragmentation increases.

Principles serve a fundamentally different purpose. They act as a shared compass for decision-making. They do not prescribe exact solutions, and they do not eliminate trade-offs. Instead, they define the boundaries within which solutions must fit. When trade-offs are inevitable, and they always are, principles help teams choose coherently, even when they disagree. They make architectural intent explicit and transferable, rather than implicit and dependent on a few individuals.

In the context of a platform, principles are even more critical. A platform is not built for a single use case or a single team. It must support many teams, diverse levels of maturity, evolving needs, and future scenarios that cannot be fully anticipated. This means the platform cannot rely on frozen assumptions about technology choices, organizational structures, or usage patterns. Any assumption hardcoded into the platform today is a constraint imposed on the organization tomorrow.

Principles provide the abstraction layer that allows the platform to adapt without losing its identity. They define what the platform is *for*, even as the way it fulfills that purpose changes over time. They allow the platform to evolve without being reinvented every few years.

For a Data Product Management Platform, principles play an additional and crucial role: they protect autonomy without sacrificing coherence. They ensure that decentralization does not degrade into chaos and that governance does not regress into control. They clarify what must remain stable as everything else changes: ownership boundaries, lifecycle semantics, integration models, and separation of responsibilities.

When these elements are not anchored in principles, organizations oscillate between extremes. They swing from centralization to decentralization, from freedom to restriction, from innovation to control. Each swing promises to fix the problems of the previous one, and each creates new problems in turn. Principles are what break this cycle.

This chapter introduces the architectural principles that underpin the platform. They are not abstract ideals or academic constructs. They are grounded in real constraints observed in large, distributed data organizations and in repeated failure modes seen when platforms grow without a clear architectural backbone. They exist to make future decisions easier, not harder.

Evolvable by Design

We live in a time where the pace of technological change has become almost violent in its acceleration, and static platforms are dead platforms, even if they do not know it yet. Every platform is born into a specific context: a dominant architectural style, a preferred toolchain, a prevailing organizational model. At birth, these assumptions feel stable. They rarely are.

Over the last fifteen years alone, we have witnessed successive paradigm shifts in data architecture: from monolithic data warehouses to data lakes, from Lakehouse to Data Mesh, and now towards Data Fabric and AI-driven systems. Each wave promised simplification and delivered a new layer of complexity. Each step forward left something behind: integrations that no longer worked, pipelines that had to be rebuilt, metadata that drifted out of sync, governance processes that could not keep up.

Many organizations are still carrying technical and organizational debt from the Hadoop era, while simultaneously building tomorrow's debt by hardcoding today's assumptions into their platforms. In this environment, a platform designed around a fixed worldview does not survive change; it resists it, and when that resistance breaks, the platform becomes the very bottleneck it was meant to eliminate. Designing for evolvability means accepting a hard truth:

We cannot predict the future.

We do not know which technologies will dominate, how teams will be organized, or which execution models will matter tomorrow. What we do know is that change will happen. Evolvability, therefore, cannot be treated as a nice-to-have; it must be a core design principle.

Just as cloud-native systems emphasize elasticity, internal platforms must emphasize adaptability: to new patterns, new technologies, and new ways of working. Being evolvable does not mean being reactive or loose. It means being intentional about flexibility. It means separating intent from implementation, encoding principles instead of tools, and avoiding hardcoded assumptions about storage, execution, or delivery patterns.

Data Product Management, like DevOps,
is a way of working rather than a technology choice.

It applies whether data products are built with SQL, APIs, notebooks, event streams, semantic graphs, or AI agents orchestrating microservices. The platform must not dictate how data products are implemented or which tools they use. It must persist while everything else changes, because regardless of the paradigm, organizations will always need to engineer processes, codify standards and contracts, govern behavior and execution, provide self-service experiences, and automate compliance and feedback loops.

An evolvable platform survives paradigm shifts not by chasing trends, but by remaining agnostic enough to accommodate them. Data Mesh, Data Fabric, and AI agents are not reasons to rebuild the platform; they are test cases for whether it was designed to evolve in the first place. If adopting a new paradigm requires dismantling the platform, then the platform was never truly enabling. It was merely aligned with the present. The only way to avoid obsolescence is to bet on change itself, to design platforms that absorb change instead of crumbling under it, and to accept that the future will belong to those who can adapt fastest, with the least friction.

Don't Over Define the Data Product

If you ask ten different organizations what a Data Product is, you will likely get ten different answers—and, in most cases, they will all be valid. Some organizations think of Data Products as well-modeled analytical tables, others as APIs; some focus on batch pipelines, others on streaming; some include machine learning models or real-time dashboards, while others treat Data Products as logical constructs that primarily define semantic meaning across domains, regardless of how data is ultimately served. This diversity is not a problem. It is the point.

A Data Product is not a fixed architecture. It is a flexible abstraction that must evolve alongside the organization, its maturity, its use cases, and its technology landscape. Problems arise when organizations try to freeze that abstraction too early.

When we talk about *over defining* Data Products, we are not referring to their external contracts. Quite the opposite. External contracts—schemas, semantics, quality guarantees, behavioral expectations—must be clearly defined and stable. They are what make Data Products consumable, interoperable, and trustworthy. What should *not* be over defined is the **internal architecture** of a

Data Product: how it is built, which technologies it uses, how logic is organized internally, or which execution patterns are adopted.

One of the fastest ways to kill evolvability is to hardcode strong architectural opinions into the inner structure of Data Products. The temptation is understandable. Organizations want clarity, architects want consistency, and platforms want a clean, uniform model. The result is often a precise definition that gets enforced everywhere, embedded into data models, user interfaces, validation rules, and automation flows.

As soon as the organization grows, matures, or diversifies its use cases, the cracks begin to show. Some teams need batch-oriented products, others need streaming. Some expose tables, others APIs. Some embed machine learning logic, others only curate and expose semantics. The internal architecture that once felt elegant becomes either too restrictive or so overloaded with exceptions that it loses coherence.

This is not a new phenomenon. We have seen it repeatedly in well-intentioned but ultimately harmful over-opinionated architectural patterns. WSDL and SOAP promised standardized, contract-first web services, until verbosity and rigid tooling made them unmanageable at scale. OSGi introduced a powerful modular system in the Java ecosystem, but its operational complexity locked teams into patterns that aged poorly. Strictly normalized 3NF data warehouses were once the gold standard, only to become rigid, expensive to evolve, and disconnected from real analytical needs. ETL-centric architectures dominated for years, until streaming and ELT emerged and exposed them as bottlenecks.

The common thread across all these examples is the same: strong assumptions were baked into internal architectures and tooling, based on the idea that one shape would fit all future needs. Reality inevitably diverged, and friction followed.

Maturity plays a crucial role here. In the early stages of a transformation, simplicity matters more than completeness. Many organizations adopting Data Product practices will start with a pragmatic definition—perhaps a curated set of tables with ownership and basic metadata—and that is entirely appropriate. Over time, however, new requirements naturally emerge: real-time ingestion, streaming outputs, low-latency APIs, event-driven delivery, machine learning artifacts, stricter SLAs, stronger security guarantees, regulatory constraints, or even data monetization and external exposure.

Governance evolves as well. What starts as manual review gradually becomes policy-as-code, automated validation, and runtime enforcement. Trying to impose all of this upfront does not create alignment; it creates resistance. You cannot meaningfully introduce data contracts when deployments are still manual. You cannot talk about circuit breakers and observability when nobody owns the pipeline. You cannot enforce high SLAs if data still moves through spreadsheets. Complexity must follow maturity, not precede it.

An enabling platform must therefore define Data Products in a way that allows their internal architecture to evolve over time, without breaking existing guarantees. It should support incremental sophistication: starting from simple descriptors, then validating metadata completeness, then introducing automated policies, then enforcing contracts, then measuring runtime behavior, and eventually orchestrating recovery and resilience mechanisms. Each step must build on the previous one, without forcing teams to adopt patterns that feel premature or disconnected from their current reality.

The moment a platform hardcodes internal architectural choices that feel excessive or foreign, it loses its users. Teams will resist, build shadow systems, bypass guardrails, or disengage altogether. This is not a technical failure; it is a social one. People reject platforms that replace their judgment with someone else's assumptions.

When platforms over define the internal architecture of Data Products, they confuse governance with rigidity and optimize for uniformity instead of adaptability. An enabling platform takes the opposite approach. It defines Data Products in a way that preserves stable external contracts, while leaving room for internal evolution. It respects domain context, supports multiple architectural styles, and allows maturity to grow naturally over time.

Only in this way can Data Products fulfill their real promise: not as fixed units of structure, but as evolving units of value.

Separation of Control Plane and Data Plane

If you look at the most resilient, scalable, and evolvable architectures in modern computing—from telecom networks to Kubernetes—they all have a clear separation between the Control Plane and the data, or user, plane. This separation is not a theoretical preference or an aesthetic choice. It is one of the main reasons these systems remain governable, maintainable, and adaptable over time.

In data platforms, however, this boundary is often blurred. This happens especially in internal platforms that try to "simplify" the user experience by doing everything themselves. In doing so, they unintentionally violate one of the most important architectural principles available to us. At its core, the rule is simple:

Governance is not execution.

The Control Plane is where intent, rules, and coordination live. It defines how the organization wants data products to be built, owned, governed, and evolved. The Control Plane encodes the way of working. This is where guardrails are defined, quality gates are enforced, and automation supports lifecycle transitions. The Control Plane is concerned with *what should happen*, *under which constraints*, and *who is accountable*, but it never touches the data itself.

In practical terms, the Control Plane manages descriptors, metadata, ownership models, documentation, software definitions, and infrastructure specifications. It applies governance policies such as metadata completeness, contract validation, or compliance checks. It automates versioning, promotion, deprecation, and other lifecycle events. It tracks dependencies between data products and reacts to governance or change-management events. All of this happens without reading a record, running a query, or executing a transformation.

This is why the Control Plane can be thought of as the operating system of the data ecosystem. It defines behavior and enforces consistency, but it does not execute workloads.

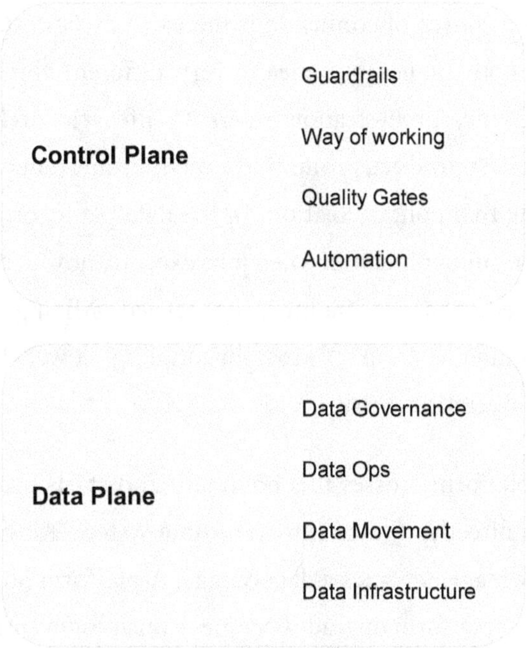

The data plane, by contrast, is where data is actually handled. This is where data is ingested, processed, transformed, queried, and served in the data plane. Pipelines built with Spark, dbt, Flink, or custom code live here. Storage systems, databases, query engines, streaming platforms, APIs, and runtime infrastructure all belong to the data plane. If a tool reads data, moves it, transforms it, or exposes it to consumers, it is part of this layer.

Data orchestration also belongs here. Scheduling, triggering, retries, and dependency management of real workloads are handled by tools such as Airflow, Dagster, or Argo Workflows. Execution logic lives here, and operational failures occur in this layer.

A common source of confusion is the word *orchestration*, which exists in both planes but means very different things. In the Control Plane, orchestration refers to lifecycle orchestration: creating a data product, promoting a version, enforcing a contract, or reacting to a policy violation. In the data plane, orchestration refers to running pipelines: when jobs execute, how dependencies are resolved, and how failures are retried. Mixing these two responsibilities leads directly to tight coupling, slower change, and increased operational risk.

When a platform crosses this boundary and starts orchestrating execution directly, it turns into a runtime system. At that point, a platform outage becomes a data outage. A platform bug can stop pipelines. A platform upgrade becomes a business event, requiring freezes, coordination across teams, and careful rollback planning. These are not hypothetical scenarios. They are common failure modes of internal platforms that mix control and execution.

In real organizations, this shows up in familiar ways: platforms embedding their own schedulers that cannot express domain-specific logic; runtime contract checks implemented inside shared APIs that introduce latency and break SLAs; platform upgrades that require weeks of coordination across dozens of teams. These are not edge cases. They are symptoms of blurred layers.

Keeping the Control Plane separate avoids all of this. The platform can govern without owning runtime responsibility. Data products continue to run even if the platform is temporarily unavailable. Execution technologies can evolve independently. Failures remain contained within the data plane. Platform upgrades become low-risk operations rather than organization-wide events. Teams can adopt new tools and patterns without waiting for the platform to "support" them.

A well-designed Data Product Management Platform therefore stays firmly in the Control Plane. It validates descriptors, schemas, metadata, and contracts. It applies computational policies at deploy time and, where appropriate, evaluates runtime signals without executing workloads. It exposes APIs for versioning, lifecycle transitions, and ownership. It generates templates and blueprints for execution patterns, but it does not run them. It tracks compliance and dependencies without becoming part of the runtime. What it must not do is:

- Schedule pipelines.
- Execute transformations.
- Serve data.

- Manage delivery endpoints.
- Become a hard dependency for data consumption.

Integration with the data plane should happen through explicit boundaries: injecting metadata into CI/CD pipelines, triggering external orchestrators via APIs or webhooks, or observing contract breaches without owning recovery logic.

Data products should keep running even if the Data Product Management platform is down.

This separation allows governance logic and execution technology to evolve independently. It reduces blast radius, improves fault isolation, enables zero-downtime platform upgrades, and supports heterogeneous runtimes across domains. Platforms that respect this boundary remain stable in concept while flexible in implementation. Platforms that ignore it may gain short-term convenience, but they trade it for long-term fragility.

The lesson is straightforward. Stay in the Control Plane. Define guardrails, enforce quality gates, and automate lifecycle governance. Let the data plane own execution, transformation, and delivery. Only by respecting this separation can a Data Product ecosystem scale—and thrive.

Embedded Automated Governance

When we talk about governance in a Data Product Management Platform whose purpose is to enable multiple teams to operate autonomously across the entire data product lifecycle, a few fundamentals need to be made explicit. Autonomy is never free. It always comes with responsibility. If autonomy is not paired with a shared and enforceable set of rules, it does not lead to empowerment; it leads to fragmentation and, eventually, chaos.

The parallel with how a society works is useful here. Individuals enjoy a high degree of freedom, but that freedom exists within a framework of rules designed to protect the freedom of others and to ensure that the system as a whole can function. Different institutions define and enforce those rules within clear scopes. A data product management platform operates in much the same way. It must define the conditions under which teams can act independently, while also ensuring that the overall ecosystem remains stable, sustainable, and fair.

In any society, members receive services and autonomy in exchange for accepting a set of rules. In return, the system has a responsibility of its own: the rules must be reasonable, the services must provide real value, and individual autonomy must be protected rather than gradually eroded. When rules become arbitrary or services stop being useful, people either stop complying or start working around the system. The exact same dynamic plays out in data platforms.

One of the core responsibilities of a Data Product Management Platform is therefore to ensure that everyone respects the rules and that no one's behavior can reduce the autonomy of others. In data terms, this means protecting shared practices, shared infrastructure, and shared trust. It requires general rules that safeguard the organization's data management approach, as well as specific safeguards that prevent the negligence or shortcuts of one team from propagating issues across the entire ecosystem.

This is where governance becomes essential. And not just data governance in the narrow sense. A platform must support governance at multiple, interconnected levels. Architectural governance keeps integration costs under control and prevents divergence that would make systems impossible to evolve. Process governance ensures that decisions, changes, and responsibilities remain traceable, which becomes critical in audits or incident investigations. Data-level governance protects sensitive information, enforces security and compliance requirements, and ensures that data remains intelligible and usable for consumers. Treating these dimensions in isolation does not work, because in practice they influence each other continuously.

The need for governance becomes even more acute when data use cases are interdependent and owned by different teams or departments. In such an environment, accountability is not optional. Teams must remain accountable for what they promise, especially in terms of data quality, availability, and behavioral guarantees. Without clear accountability, a single weak link can degrade the reliability of multiple downstream use cases, eroding trust across the organization and undermining the entire data ecosystem.

For these reasons, governance in a Data Product Management Platform cannot rely on documents, manual reviews, or good intentions. That approach does not scale. Governance must be embedded into the system and automated by design. Only embedded and automated governance can support a healthy ecosystem of people, processes, and technologies—one that protects autonomy, reduces friction, and remains sustainable as the organization grows and evolves.

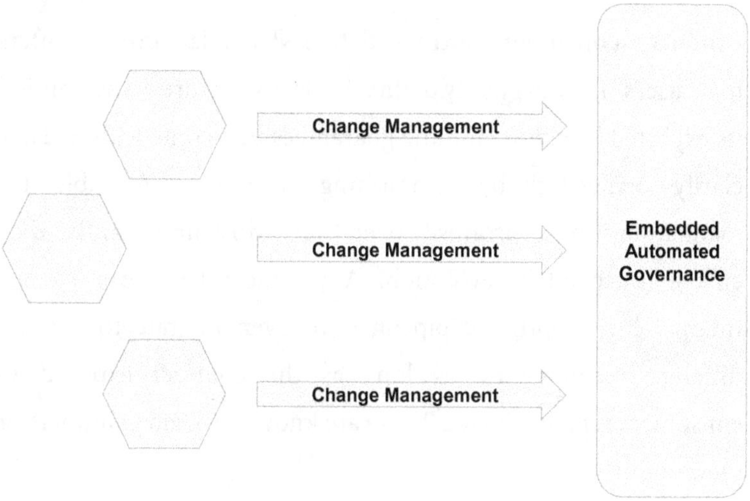

Contracts First Approach

In a world where change is constant, very few things can realistically remain stable over time. Technologies evolve, architectures shift, organizational boundaries move, and even the way teams work together changes as companies grow and adapt. Trying to freeze any of these elements is a losing battle. There is, however, one category of abstraction that *must* remain stable if a system is to hold together: contracts.

Everything else is negotiable. Contracts are not.

At their core, contracts capture promises. They define what one party can reliably expect from another, regardless of how things are implemented internally. In a data product ecosystem, this idea appears in two critical places.

Producer–consumer contracts define what a data product offers to its users. They explicitly define the data structure, its semantics, its expected behavior, and the guarantees that come with it. They clarify ownership by establishing who is responsible for maintaining those promises over time. Most importantly, they enable independent evolution. A producer team can change internal logic, optimize pipelines, or even migrate to entirely different technologies, as long as the contract exposed to consumers remains intact. These are known as Data Contracts or Output Ports.

User–platform contracts serve a similar purpose, but at a different level. They define what the platform guarantees to its users: how the data product lifecycle is managed, how governance is enforced, what backward compatibility means in practice, how changes are handled, and what kind of support teams can rely on. These contracts are what turn a platform from a collection of tools into a trusted system. They set clear expectations and reduce uncertainty, both for delivery teams and for governance functions.

Together, these contracts form the only abstractions that should be treated as truly stable. Everything behind them must remain flexible.

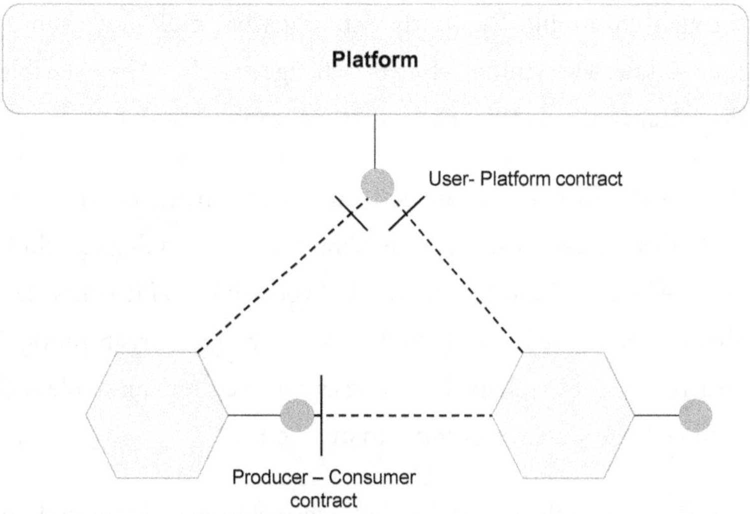

This distinction is crucial. When platforms hardcode assumptions that go beyond contracts—for example, specific technologies, architectural patterns, or implementation details—they freeze choices that will inevitably become wrong. What feels like a sensible standard today often turns into tomorrow's constraint. The result is friction, workarounds, and eventually a costly rewrite.

When contracts are explicit, enforced, and well understood, the opposite happens. Internals can evolve freely without breaking the ecosystem. Teams gain confidence to improve and innovate, knowing that as long as they respect their contracts, they will not harm others. Governance becomes enforceable without becoming intrusive, because it focuses on promises rather than implementations.

This is why contracts are so powerful. They create freedom through constraint. By clearly defining what must not change, they allow everything else to change safely. They enable decentralization without chaos and evolution without fear.

A Data Product Management Platform that treats contracts as first-class citizens can survive almost any technological shift. Storage engines can be replaced. Processing frameworks can change. New delivery patterns can emerge. Organizational structures can be reshaped. As long as contracts remain stable and enforced, the system continues to function.

A platform that does not take contracts seriously will find itself in a very different cycle. It will be constantly rebuilt, renamed, and rebranded. Each iteration will promise to fix the shortcomings of the previous one, yet the same problems will reappear, because the underlying abstraction was never stabilized.

In the long run, it is not technology that holds a data ecosystem together. It is trust. Contracts are how that trust is made explicit, operational, and sustainable.

Everything as Code

A modern platform manages many different artifacts: infrastructure definitions, transformation logic, metadata descriptors, documentation, data contracts, governance policies, and quality rules. In many organizations, these elements are handled through different systems and processes. Pipelines are written as code, metadata is edited through catalog interfaces, documentation lives in wikis, governance rules are captured in policy documents, and contracts may exist in separate registries.

This fragmentation increases platform complexity and makes governance harder to enforce consistently.

Adopting the principle of *everything as code* addresses this problem by expressing all structural artifacts of the platform as versioned, declarative definitions. Infrastructure, metadata, documentation, policies, contracts, and configuration become artifacts stored in version control and evolve through the same development workflow: pull requests, review, automated validation, and CI/CD-based promotion across environments.

In practice, *everything as code* does not mean that every contributor must write code. The principle simply means that the underlying model for authoring, change management, and release follows the same discipline used in software development. Platform teams can provide higher-level abstractions, templates, or user interfaces that remove the barrier of writing raw code while still producing structured artifacts behind the scenes. What matters is not how users interact with the system, but how the artifacts are represented and managed internally.

It is also important to distinguish between how artifacts are stored and how they are presented. The internal representation of an artifact may be a declarative definition stored in version control, but how it is visualized and consumed can vary significantly depending on the asset. Documentation may be rendered as rich pages, metadata may appear as searchable catalog entries, and governance policies may be presented as structured rules or dashboards. The platform should therefore optimize the representation of each asset for usability and discoverability while maintaining a consistent operational model behind the scenes.

When every artifact follows the same change management process, governance becomes significantly simpler. Validation no longer happens in multiple systems or through manual reviews scattered across the organization. Instead, governance rules can be enforced in a single place within the delivery pipeline. The same automated checks validate infrastructure definitions, metadata descriptors, documentation completeness, contracts, and policies before any change is promoted. Governance therefore becomes systematic rather than procedural.

For the platform itself, this principle reduces structural complexity. Instead of maintaining different management mechanisms for each asset type, the platform adopts a single operational pattern for authoring, storing, versioning, and releasing artifacts. Infrastructure definitions, metadata, documentation, and governance rules are all treated in the same way.

This consistency also makes the platform easier to evolve. Data platforms inevitably expand to include new types of artifacts: additional governance entities, semantic models, new categories of data products, or assets that did not originally exist when the platform was designed. When everything follows the same DevOps-based lifecycle, new artifacts can be introduced without introducing new operational models. Even assets composed entirely of metadata can be authored, versioned, validated, and released through the same workflow.

In practice, the platform follows a unified pattern aligned with DevOps principles: artifacts are authored as structured definitions, stored in version control, reviewed via pull requests, automatically validated, and released via CI/CD pipelines. The platform treats infrastructure, metadata, documentation, and governance artifacts equally in terms of operational management. This principle has become even more important in the era of AI-assisted development.

Modern AI tools dramatically accelerate activities that operate on code and structured artifacts: generation, refactoring, documentation, validation, review, and debugging. Developers already experience this acceleration when writing software. The same acceleration can apply to metadata, contracts, policies, and documentation—but only if these elements are expressed as structured artifacts within the same engineering lifecycle.

If metadata, documentation, or governance definitions remain trapped inside graphical interfaces, spreadsheets, or disconnected management tools, they remain largely inaccessible to the AI tooling that is transforming software engineering. If they are defined as versioned artifacts, AI can assist with their creation, suggest improvements, detect inconsistencies, generate missing documentation, and help maintain them over time.

Treating everything as code therefore unlocks the same productivity gains for the entire data product lifecycle that developers already experience in software engineering. Metadata becomes easier to create, governance becomes easier to enforce, documentation stays aligned with implementation, and the platform benefits from the accelerating capabilities of modern development tooling.

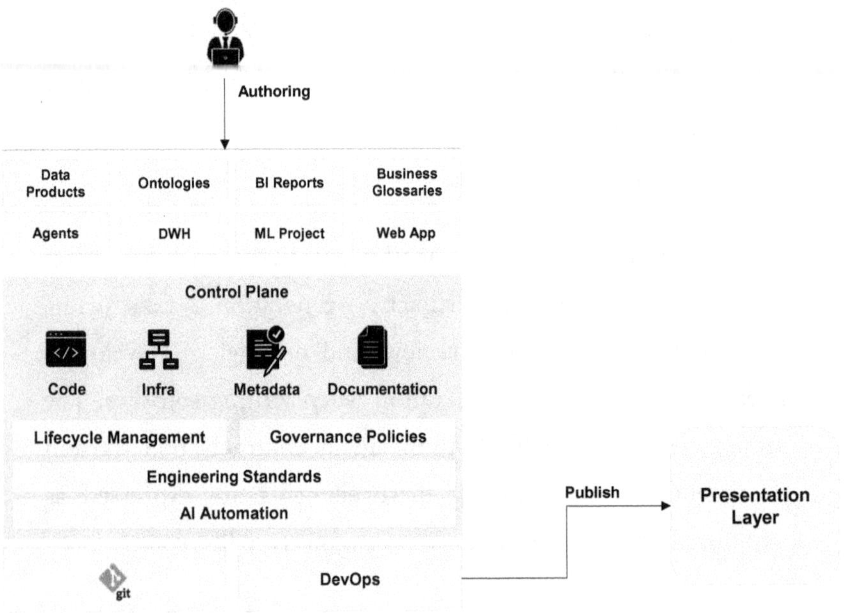

Key Takeaway

- Principles are what remain when technologies change.
- Architectures age and tools become obsolete. What endures are the principles that guided the original design choices.
- An enabling platform is not defined by its stack, but by its ability to adapt without losing coherence. Evolvability, flexibility, separation of concerns, and contract-first thinking are not optional qualities. They are the difference between a platform that grows with the organization and one that must be replaced every few years.

Only after these principles are clear does it make sense to talk about architecture.

Logical Architecture

At this point in the book, it finally makes sense to look at the platform as a system. Not as a list of tools. Not as a reference stack. But as a set of capabilities, each with a clear responsibility, and with carefully defined boundaries between them.

The architecture on the next page represents the logical architecture of a Data Product Management Platform. Logical does not mean abstract or theoretical. It means that what you see is independent of specific technologies, vendors, or deployment choices. These building blocks must exist in *some form* in any platform that wants to scale data products sustainably.

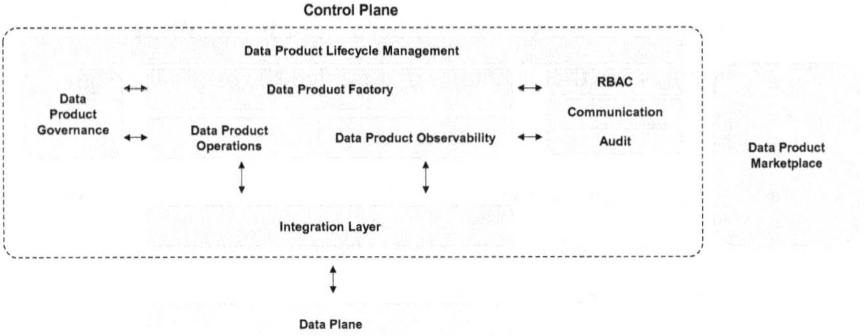

The most important thing to notice is that the architecture is explicitly organized around two planes: the Control Plane and the data plane. Everything else derives from that separation.

Let's walk through the diagram from top to bottom, and from left to right, focusing on *what each layer is responsible for*, not on *how it is implemented*. The "how" will come later.

Control Plane: Where Intent, Governance, and Lifecycle Live

The dashed box at the top of the diagram represents the Control Plane.

This is the heart of the platform. It is where intent is defined, validated, governed, and monitored. The Control Plane does not move data, does not execute pipelines, and does not serve queries. Instead, it defines *how data products are supposed to exist and behave* within the organization.

The Control Plane is composed of several tightly related capabilities and has the final goal of managing the entire Data Product Lifecycle.

Data Product Lifecycle Management

The Data Product Lifecycle Management module is where the platform orchestrates the full journey of a Data Product, from its initial idea to its retirement. While the Data Product Factory focuses on creation, this layer provides continuity. It connects all phases, stakeholders, and systems involved in the lifecycle into a single, coherent flow.

Its role is to make the lifecycle explicit, navigable, and operational. Instead of leaving teams to interpret documentation or chase approvals across disconnected systems, the platform guides them step by step. At any moment, teams know where they are, what needs to happen next, which conditions must be satisfied, and who is involved in moving forward.

This is where complexity is absorbed by the platform. Enterprise processes such as architectural reviews, governance approvals, environment provisioning, and dataset registration do not disappear, but they become orchestrated. The platform integrates with the surrounding ecosystem and turns a fragmented set of activities into a structured and visible process.

Conceptually, this module answers questions like:

- Where is my Data Product in its lifecycle?
- What are the next steps to reach production?
- Which approvals or validations are required?
- Where are the bottlenecks slowing us down?

At this level, the platform does not execute the data workload itself. It governs how the Data Product evolves over time, ensuring that every step in the lifecycle is aligned, traceable, and manageable.

Data Product Governance

Data Product Governance is responsible for defining and enforcing the shared rules of the ecosystem.

This is where architectural standards, security constraints, compliance requirements, and organizational policies are formalized. Importantly, these rules are not just written down—they are made executable.

Governance here is not an approval committee. It is a system capability that evaluates whether a data product complies with the rules required to safely participate in the ecosystem. This includes, for example:

- Architectural constraints.
- Security and privacy requirements.
- Mandatory metadata.
- Policy evaluation at deploy and runtime.

Governance in the Control Plane exists to protect the autonomy of everyone else by preventing individual actions from creating systemic risk.

Data Product Factory

The Data Product Factory is where data products are created. Its role is to reduce cognitive load for teams by providing assisted creation of data products. Instead of starting from a blank slate, teams use templates, blueprints, and guided workflows that encode best practices and governance requirements by default.

This is where autonomy becomes practical. Teams can move fast because they are not required to understand every platform rule or architectural constraint upfront. The factory embeds those rules into the creation process itself. Conceptually, the factory answers questions like:

- How do I bootstrap a new data product?
- Which components are required?
- Which standards apply?
- What does "ready to be deployed" mean?

At this level, the factory does not execute anything. It produces *intent*, not *runtime behavior*.

Data Product Operations

Once a data product exists, it must be operated across its lifecycle.

Data Product Operations is the capability responsible for managing lifecycle transitions: deploy, promote, upgrade, rollback, deprecate, and retire. This is not about running pipelines; it is about managing the state of the data product as a product.

This component ensures atomicity and accountability: when a data product changes state, all relevant aspects change together—software, metadata, contracts, and governance checks.

Operations in the Control Plane make lifecycle events explicit and auditable, rather than implicit and ad hoc.

Data Product Observability

Data Product Observability exists to build and maintain trust.

It aggregates signals about how a data product behaves over time: quality indicators, SLA compliance, contract adherence, and operational health. These signals are not just metrics for dashboards. They are inputs into governance, lifecycle decisions, and consumer trust.

Observability in the Control Plane answers questions like:

- Is this data product behaving as promised?
- Are consumers affected by upstream issues?
- Can this product still be trusted?

This is where runtime reality feeds back into governance and lifecycle management.

Cross-Cutting Capabilities: RBAC, Communication, Audit

Some capabilities cut across the entire Control Plane:

- RBAC defines who can see, change, or operate what, enforcing separation of responsibilities.
- Communication ensures that lifecycle events, governance outcomes, and incidents are surfaced to the right people at the right time.
- Audit guarantees traceability: who did what, when, and why.

These are not optional add-ons. They are foundational to operating data products in regulated, multi-team environments.

Integration Layer

At the bottom of the Control Plane sits the Integration Layer.

This is one of the most critical—and most misunderstood—components. The integration layer is the boundary between intent and execution. It is how the Control Plane interacts with the data plane without owning it. It exposes APIs, events, and hooks that allow external systems to react to lifecycle and governance decisions. Through this layer, the platform can:

- Trigger CI/CD pipelines.
- Notify external orchestrators.
- Receive observability signals.
- Propagate metadata.

Crucially, the integration layer does not execute workloads itself. It connects, it signals, it coordinates.

Data Plane: Where Execution Happens

Below the Control Plane sits the data plane. This is where data actually lives and flows. Pipelines run here. Queries execute here. Models score here. This plane includes all the technologies teams use to implement data products: processing engines, storage systems, streaming platforms, and serving layers.

The platform does not control how the data plane works. It governs *about* it, not *through* it. This separation ensures that:

- Data products continue to run even if the platform is unavailable.
- Execution technologies can evolve independently.
- Innovation in the data plane is not blocked by the platform.

The Data Product Marketplace

Finally, on the side of the Control Plane, we see the Data Product Marketplace.

The marketplace is not part of execution. It is not an inspection tool. It is the place where data products are discovered, understood, and consumed.

It exposes the output of the Control Plane—metadata, contracts, trust signals—to consumers. It turns data consumption into an explicit interaction between producers and consumers, mediated by the platform.

The marketplace is where the ecosystem becomes visible.

Putting It All Together

This logical architecture is deliberately opinionated about *responsibilities*, not technologies.

Each block exists to solve a specific class of problems. Each boundary exists to prevent coupling that would make the system fragile. Together, they form a platform that can govern data products without suffocating them, and enable autonomy without sacrificing trust.

In the next chapter, we will open each of these boxes and explore how they work in practice. But from this point on, the reader should already have a mental model: where intent lives, where execution happens, and how the two interact without collapsing into each other.

That mental model is the foundation for everything that follows.

If the logical architecture defines what the platform must do, the physical architecture defines how those responsibilities are realized in concrete, deployable components.

This translation is not neutral. The physical architecture must embody the principles established earlier. If it contradicts them, the platform will fail regardless of how elegant the logical model looks on paper.

In particular, the physical architecture of a Data Product Management Platform must be deliberately designed to support change, isolation, and independent evolution. This is not an aesthetic preference; it is a structural necessity.

Before looking at the main building blocks, it is worth restating the constraints that shape every physical design choice.

Physical Architecture

The physical architecture must embrace the principles established earlier, plus some others that are more on the technical side:

- **Technology agnostic by default.** The platform must avoid tight coupling to a single vendor's stack, execution engine, or infrastructure provider. Physical components should depend on abstractions, APIs, and contracts rather than concrete technologies, to prevent lock-in and allow substitution over time.

- **Strict separation of Control Plane and data plane.** The platform governs, automates, validates, and observes—but it does not execute the user's pipelines or serve their data. This separation must be visible in deployment boundaries, not just in diagrams.
- **Composable and extensible.** Capabilities must be addable, replaceable, and evolvable without rewriting the entire system. The platform must tolerate growth, experimentation, and partial adoption.
- **Integration-first.** The platform does not live in isolation. APIs, events, webhooks, and adapters are not secondary concerns; they are the primary means by which the platform interacts with the enterprise ecosystem.

These constraints strongly influence one key architectural decision.

Why a Microservices Architecture is Important

Given the clarity of responsibilities and bounded contexts in the logical architecture, a monolithic physical architecture would be a contradiction.

Each capability in the Control Plane—governance, factory, lifecycle operations, observability, marketplace, integration—

represents a distinct bounded context with its own data, behavior, and evolution cadence. Trying to implement these concerns inside a single deployable unit inevitably leads to tight coupling, shared state, and coordination overhead.

A microservices-based physical architecture is therefore not a fashionable choice. It is the natural consequence of the problem we are solving.

Microservices allow the platform to reflect, at runtime, the same separation of responsibilities expressed in the logical model.

The benefits are concrete:

- **Independent evolution**. Each capability can evolve without forcing coordinated releases across the entire platform.

- **Fault isolation**. A failure in observability or notification does not bring down lifecycle management or governance enforcement.

- **Modularity and composability**. New capabilities can be introduced incrementally, without destabilizing existing ones.

- **Technology flexibility**. Different services can adopt different internal technologies if needed, without imposing them globally.

- **Organizational alignment**. Teams can own services aligned with clear responsibilities, reducing cognitive and coordination load.

Most importantly, microservices prevent a subtle but dangerous failure mode: the platform becoming a single point of coupling for everything.

With these constraints in mind, the physical architecture typically materializes into a small number of clearly separated component groups.

Control Plane Services

The Control Plane is implemented as a set of cooperating microservices, each responsible for a specific aspect of intent, governance, or lifecycle.

These services typically include:

- Lifecycle and state management services, responsible for managing data product states and transitions.
- Metadata and descriptor services, storing and validating declarative definitions.
- Governance and policy engines, evaluating architectural, security, and compliance rules.
- Template and blueprint services, providing standardized creation patterns.

- Observability aggregation services, collecting and interpreting behavioral signals.
- Marketplace services, exposing curated views for discovery and consumption.

These services operate on declarative intent, not on data flows. They decide *whether* something is allowed, *when* it can happen, and *under which conditions*—but they do not execute workloads themselves.

Execution Contexts (Data Plane)

Execution contexts live outside the platform. They include the user's pipelines, storage systems, streaming platforms, serving layers, and runtime environments. These systems are owned by data product teams and evolve according to their needs.

The platform interacts with these contexts indirectly, through contracts, metadata, events, and policy enforcement hooks. It can observe behavior and block non-compliant changes, but it does not become a runtime dependency. This design ensures a critical property:

If the platform is unavailable, data products keep running.

Avoiding runtime lock-in is not a theoretical concern. Platforms that violate this boundary often become impossible to upgrade, impossible to replace, and too risky to touch.

Integration Components

Integration components form the connective tissue of the platform.

These are services and adapters responsible for connecting the Control Plane to the surrounding enterprise ecosystem, including:

- CI/CD systems.
- Identity providers.
- Infrastructure provisioning tools.
- External orchestrators.
- Monitoring and alerting systems.
- Existing data catalogs or registries.

These integrations should be explicit, versioned, and replaceable. Adapters should absorb external variability so that the core platform remains stable even as the ecosystem changes.

This is where integration-first design becomes tangible.

User Interfaces and APIs

Finally, the platform exposes its capabilities through user-facing interfaces. This includes:

- Web UIs tailored to different personas.
- APIs for automation and integration.
- Event streams for asynchronous interaction.

These interfaces are not just access points. They are part of the platform's ergonomics. Their primary role is to reduce cognitive load, match user skill levels, and make the "right thing" the easy thing.

A microservices architecture enables these interfaces to evolve independently, without forcing changes deep into the platform core.

Why this Architecture Scales

By mapping clear logical responsibilities onto independent physical components, the platform gains a crucial property: structural resilience. Capabilities can evolve without global rewrites. Technologies can change without breaking intent. New patterns can be introduced without invalidating existing data products. Most importantly, the platform remains an enabler rather than a bottleneck. This is not about adopting microservices for their own sake. It is about building a system whose physical shape reflects its conceptual boundaries, and whose structure absorbs change instead of resisting it.

Platform Metamodel

A central design principle is **future-proofing** the platform by making its **metamodel** evolvable.

When we start, the focus is often on **data products**. But the same decentralization and governance principles might soon apply to:

- AI Agents that automate business tasks.
- BI Reporting Packages with strict ownership.
- Operational APIs exposed across domains.

If the platform hardcodes "data products" as the only type of managed system, we will eventually face painful refactoring and confusing terminology for users. Instead, we should define a **generic architecture/practice metamodel**.

Architecture/Practice Metamodel

One of the core principles in designing a truly durable Data Product Management Platform is its ability to **evolve over time**. Many projects are born with a narrow focus on the "here and now": today the scope is data products, so the model is designed to describe only data products. It feels like a safe shortcut, but it becomes an expensive trap as soon as the environment changes.

Change is not a remote possibility—it is a certainty.

History in IT proves the point. In just a few years, we have shifted from centralized to decentralized models, witnessed the rise of cloud computing, adopted DevOps and DataOps, and now we are racing into the age of AI agents. Each shift brings new types of systems to govern and new interoperability needs.

Imagine that today we only have data products. Two years from now, the organization may want to apply the same decentralization and governance principles to AI agents, or to BI reporting packages that require a lifecycle, ownership, and policies similar to data products. If the platform has been designed with the assumption that there is only one kind of "governed entity," we will be forced to stretch the concept of "data product" until it loses its meaning—cluttering it with exceptions, overloading its definition, and creating confusion for users who no longer recognize their own terms.

The way to avoid this trap is to define an **architectural and practice metamodel** that is generic enough to represent any type of system we might want to introduce in the future. In such a metamodel, data products are simply one possible "system type." Others can be introduced gradually—agents, reporting packages, public APIs—each with their own instances, their own rules, and their own ownership models.

A generic metamodel unlocks three key capabilities. First, **governance becomes selective and targeted**: a policy can apply only to certain system types. The rules I impose on a data product, such as strict adherence to a data contract, might be completely different from those for an AI agent, which may require explainability and auditability checks, or from those for a reporting package, where the priority is the consistency of KPIs and certification of sources.

Second, the metamodel can describe the relationships and interactions between different types of systems. I can establish, for instance, that an AI agent is not allowed to read data directly from a reporting package, but only from a certified data product. Or that certain reporting packages may aggregate from multiple sources, but must respect a clear chain of ownership and traceability.

Third, the **ownership model** becomes adaptable. A data product might have a Data Product Owner and belong to a formal business domain. An AI agent might be owned by a technical department or a cross-functional team. A reporting package might be tied to a business process and governed by business stakeholders. Over time, even the ownership model for data products themselves can evolve, adapting to organizational changes without breaking the platform.

This elasticity is critical to avoid **breaking changes** in the specification. With a generic metamodel, introducing a new system type does not require rewriting the definition of a data product or retrofitting dozens of templates and policies. The platform evolves gradually, stays compatible, and gives users the continuity they need to keep working without disruption. In essence, the metamodel is the language the platform uses to **think about** the systems it governs. If this language is rich, flexible, and open to new vocabulary, the platform can accompany the organization for many years without having to redefine itself every time technology or business priorities shift. It is the difference between laying a fixed-gauge track and designing a network that can accommodate any kind of train—present and future. We begin with a small vocabulary:

- **System Type** and **System Instance**: a type describes a family; an instance is a concrete system created by a team. Think “Data Product,” “Agent,” or “Reporting Package” as system types; “Customer-360,” “Pricing Assistant,” or “Executive Sales Reports” as instances.

- **Domain Type** and **Domain Instance**: we organize systems inside business domains. ”Sales” is a domain type; “EU Sales” is a domain instance.

- **Owner Type** and **Owner**: ownership can vary. A “Data Product Owner,” a “Department Owner,” or a “Process Owner” are owner types; actual people or groups are owners.

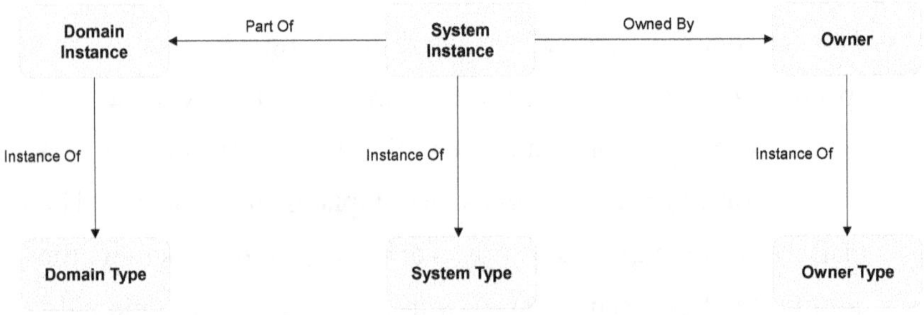

At this stage, we only express three relationships:

- A System Instance is Part Of a Domain Instance.
- A System Instance is Owned By an Owner.
- Each box is an Instance Of its corresponding type.

This simple shape lets us define multiple **system types**—Data Product, Agent, Reporting Package—and create as many instances as we need, with clear ownership and domain boundaries.

Concrete example

- System Type: Data Product → System Instance: "Customer-360."
- Domain Type: Sales → Domain Instance: "EU Sales."
- Owner Type: Data Product Owner → Owner: "Alex Rossi."

This is the first step towards a platform ontology. Now we evolve the metamodel to encode two powerful ideas:

1. **Policies apply to types, not to everything.** A **Governance Policy** is **Applicable To** one or more **System Types**. This makes governance selective and precise. The policies for a data product—data contracts, freshness, lineage—can differ from those for an agent—explainability, prompt logging—or a reporting package—KPI certification.
2. **"Read From" expresses who can consume whom.** We attach a **Read From** rule to the **System Type** to describe allowed dependencies between types. If you have invested in data products, you might decide that agents **must** read from data products, not from ad-hoc datasets

or dashboards. A reporting package may read only from certified data products.

Concrete examples

- Policy targeting: "Breaking-change detection" applies to **Data Product**. "Agent action logging" applies to **Agent**.
- Read From: **Agent** → may read from **Data Product** only. **Reporting Package** → may read from **Data Product** and other **Reporting Package** types that are certified.

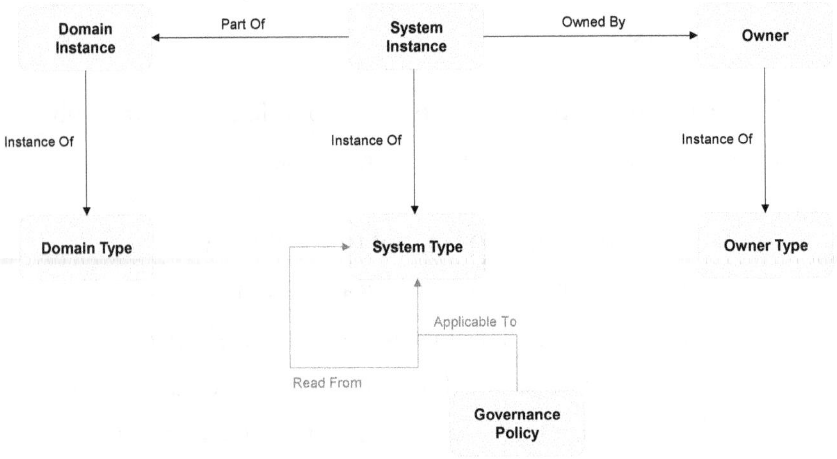

Once this structure exists, introducing a new **System Type** does not force us to change the data product specification. We simply add a type and wire it into policies and "Read From" rules.

Concrete example

Tomorrow you introduce a **RAG Service** as a new System Type. You declare:

- **Policies**: "PII redaction at prompt time," "Knowledge source attribution."
- **Read From**: RAG Service → may read from **Data Product** and from a certified **Knowledge Base** type. No breaking changes, no template rewrites, no user confusion.

Ownership can change across system types and over time. A data product might have a **Data Product Owner** and belong to a business domain. An agent might be owned by a cross-functional **Automation Team** and sit in a departmental domain. A reporting package might be owned by a **Finance Process Owner**. The metamodel embraces these differences without forcing every system into the same ownership model.

Concrete example

- "Customer-360" (Data Product) → owned by a Data Product Owner in **EU Sales**.
- "Pricing Assistant" (Agent) → owned by the **Commercial Ops** team in **Global Sales**.
- "Executive Sales Reports" (Reporting Package) → owned by the **SVP Finance** under **Corporate Finance**.

With this metamodel in place, the platform remains flexible:

- You tailor **policies** per type, so governance feels relevant, not generic.

- You shape **interactions** with **Read From** rules, so data flows follow your architectural intent.

- You evolve **ownership** without churn, reflecting how the organization actually works.

Most importantly, you can keep adding new kinds of systems—APIs, knowledge bases, real-time decisioning services—without rewriting the definition of a data product or causing breaking changes. The platform grows by adding new words to its language, not by redefining old ones.

It is worth explicitly acknowledging the research work of David Greco, a colleague of mine, who pioneered many of the ideas behind the concept of a *software-defined platform*. In his work on the *Ontology-Based Generation of Data Platform Assets*, David explored how platform capabilities, standards, and behaviors can be expressed declaratively and enforced through software rather than documentation or manual processes. This research anticipated a shift away from static catalogs and hard-coded platforms toward systems that can be shaped, evolved, and governed through explicit definitions and executable rules.

That work laid important conceptual foundations for treating platforms not as fixed technical stacks, but as adaptable systems whose structure and governance are defined in code. Many of the principles discussed in this book—such as separating intent from implementation, embedding governance into delivery, and enabling controlled evolution at scale—build on the same line of thinking. While the implementations may differ, the underlying idea remains the same:

> *Platforms should be programmable, policy-driven, and resilient to change by design, rather than rigid architectures frozen in time.*

Data Product Metamodel

When we talk about evolvability in a platform, we often focus on the data products themselves. But there is another, equally important layer that must evolve over time: the **data product metamodel**, or specification. This is the schema that defines how we describe, structure, and govern data products. If the metamodel is too rigid, the platform will eventually hit a wall. If it is open and adaptable, the platform will be able to accommodate new business requirements, regulatory demands, and industry practices without disruption.

What is a Data Product Metamodel?

At its core, the metamodel is a specification. It describes the shape of a data product descriptor, ensuring that every product is documented in a consistent and conformed way. Think of the descriptor as the "instance" and the metamodel as the "blueprint." The descriptor is what teams fill in when they define a particular data product. The metamodel is the structure that guarantees those descriptors can be interpreted, validated, and surfaced in the marketplace. A well-designed descriptor covers multiple perspectives of the product:

- **Business**. Purpose, expected value, who it serves, what it does not provide.
- **Technical**. Structure of the information, input and output ports, expected formats.
- **Infrastructure**. How the product is deployed and operated.
- **Security and compliance**. How sensitive information is protected, how access is managed.

These are only examples; in practice, the descriptor may also include metadata on lifecycle stage, cost allocation, observability endpoints, and much more. The important point is that the metamodel defines which traits are mandatory, which are optional, and how they should be expressed.

Why Evolvability Matters

Many vendors and initiatives in the market today promote a fixed specification for data products. Yet the reality inside organizations tells a different story. Most large companies already customize their own specifications, extending them with internal fields and practices. They do this not out of whim but because **business priorities evolve faster than industry standards**.

Consider the banking sector. Regulations such as DORA have already come into force, and they impose specific requirements on IT systems—including data products. At the time of writing, most public specifications for data products do not account for DORA's semantics or controls. A bank cannot afford to wait for a generic specification committee to eventually add them. They must evolve their own data product specification immediately, to remain compliant. This is not an exception but the rule: every regulated industry faces similar pressures.

If the platform cannot absorb these extensions quickly, the organization is forced into shadow practices: side documents, disconnected tools, or duplicated registries. In contrast, a platform that allows incremental, backward-compatible evolution of the specification becomes a strategic asset. It supports change without disruption and keeps the official marketplace in step with reality.

Supporting Multiple Versions

Another critical capability is versioning. Once a company has hundreds of data products registered, any change to the specification cannot be applied overnight. It requires change management, coordination across teams, and staged adoption. For this reason, the platform must support multiple specification versions at the same time. Older data products continue to operate under their current descriptor, while new or upgraded products adopt the extended specification. Over time, the organization converges, but without breaking continuity.

No Hardcoding in the Platform

To make this work, the platform must avoid hardcoding the semantics of the specification. If user interfaces, forms, and marketplace pages are rigidly tied to a fixed schema, every evolution becomes a development project. Instead, the UI should be driven by configuration: forms, validations, and representations adapt automatically as the specification evolves. This ensures that the platform does not become a barrier but an enabler of progress.

Key Takeaways

- A good architecture absorbs change instead of resisting it.
- When intent is clear and principles are respected, architecture becomes a stabilizing force rather than a constraint. Logical capabilities guide structure. Physical design prioritizes replaceability. The metamodel governs diversity without freezing it.
- At this point, the platform is no longer a collection of tools. It is a system that encodes how the organization wants to build, govern, and evolve data products—today and tomorrow.

In the next chapter, we will focus on how this architecture comes to life in practice, and how teams interact with it day by day without even realizing that governance is happening at all.

FOUR

Platform Architectural Deep Dive

From definition to runtime and back

Up to this point, we have described the platform in terms of principles, responsibilities, and structural boundaries. We have talked about intent, governance, lifecycle, and architecture. Now it is time to look at how these ideas materialize into concrete platform capabilities.

This chapter of the book focuses on **operating data products at scale**. Not in the sense of running pipelines or tuning performance, but in the sense of enabling many teams to create, evolve, consume, and trust data products over time, without the system collapsing under its own complexity.

A data product does not exist just because data flows through a pipeline. It exists only if it can be **created intentionally**, **operated safely**, **observed reliably**, and **consumed with trust**. Each of these aspects is handled by a specific module of the platform. Together, these modules form the operational backbone of the Data Product Management Platform.

The Data Product Lifecycle Management

The Data Product lifecycle is where the platform ensures continuity across the entire journey of a Data Product, from initial idea to retirement. While other modules focus on specific capabilities, this one connects everything together. It provides the structure that allows a Data Product to evolve in a controlled, visible, and repeatable way.

When we talk about Data Products, we often simplify the conversation too much. We describe them as datasets, pipelines, or interfaces. But in an enterprise context, a Data Product is none of those things in isolation. It is a software application that produces, exposes, and governs data. Once we accept this, one consequence becomes unavoidable: we must treat it as any other enterprise-grade software system, with a defined lifecycle.

Why the Lifecycle Matters

In large organizations, nothing goes from idea to production in a straight line. A Data Product must navigate a complex landscape of approvals, validations, and integrations before it can create any value. Budget approvals, architectural reviews, data governance checks, security validations, and sometimes even ethics or AI governance boards all become part of the journey.

What starts as a simple idea quickly becomes a long chain of steps involving multiple stakeholders, each responsible for protecting a different aspect of the organization. This is not an exception. It is the norm.

The journey typically moves from business requirements and architectural blueprints, through multiple governance boards, into environment provisioning, dataset registration, cloud onboarding, and testing across different stages. Only after a long sequence of transitions does the Data Product reach production. Even then, the journey continues with monitoring, feedback collection, incident management, and continuous upgrades, until eventually the Data Product is retired in a controlled way.

The problem is not that these processes exist. The problem is how they are experienced.

From the perspective of a Data Product team, the journey is often opaque. After one approval, the next step is unclear. Teams are left asking what to do next, who to contact, what is blocking them, and why progress is so slow. The lifecycle lives in documents, spreadsheets, and fragmented systems. It does not guide behavior.

From the perspective of the platform team, the situation is equally frustrating. The platform is often blamed for slow adoption or poor experience. In reality, the platform is being confused with the entire journey from zero to one. The friction does not come from the platform itself, but from the lack of orchestration across the lifecycle.

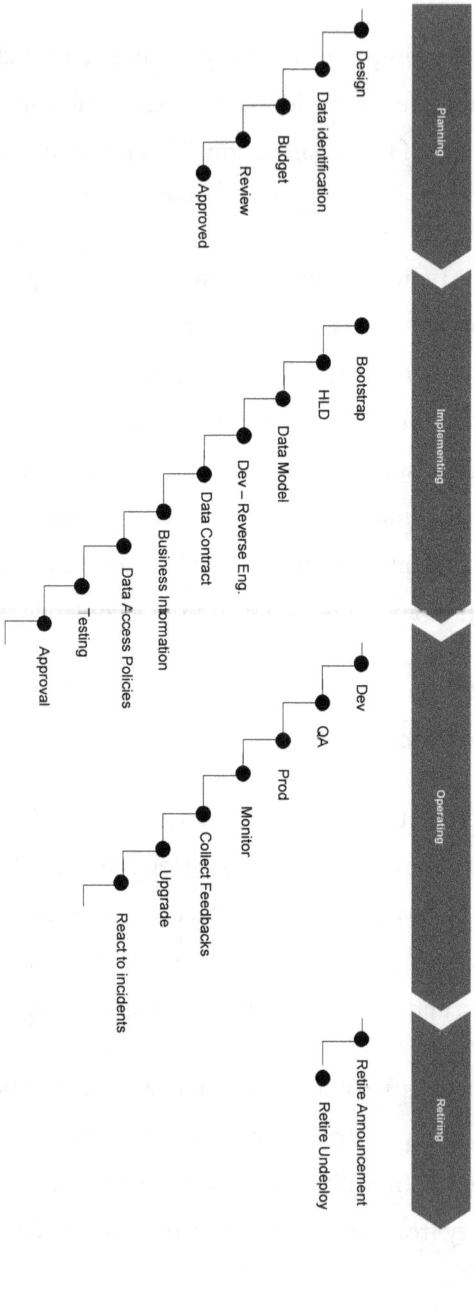

This confusion is one of the most common failure patterns in enterprise data initiatives.

The Role of the Platform

The platform is not just a collection of tools. Its role is to orchestrate and streamline the Data Product lifecycle end-to-end.

This changes the nature of the problem.

Instead of leaving the lifecycle fragmented across documents and systems, the platform turns it into a living, executable process. It makes the journey visible, navigable, and actionable.

At any moment, a Data Product team should know exactly where they are in the lifecycle, what the next step is, which conditions must be satisfied, and which stakeholder is responsible for moving things forward. The platform becomes a guide.

This is what enables real self-service. Without this guidance, self-service reduces to infrastructure provisioning, shifting complexity onto teams instead of removing it. At the same time, the platform provides visibility for the platform team. Adoption becomes measurable. Lead time becomes observable. Bottlenecks become identifiable. It becomes possible to understand where teams are getting stuck and why. The lifecycle of each Data Product can be inspected individually or analyzed across the organization.

This is how you move from perception to control.

From Phases to Workflows

At a high level, every Data Product follows four macro phases: planning, implementing, operating, and retiring.

Planning is where intent is defined. Business requirements are clarified, data is identified, budgets are estimated, and initial designs are shaped. Governance and architecture stakeholders are already involved, influencing decisions before any implementation starts.

Implementing is where the Data Product is built. Architectures are formalized, data models are defined, Data Contracts are established, access policies are configured, and testing ensures that everything behaves as expected. This is also where enterprise processes accumulate, from environment provisioning to approvals and registrations.

Operating is where the Data Product lives. It runs in production, is monitored, evolves over time, collects feedback, and reacts to incidents. This phase is continuous and dynamic.

Retiring is where the Data Product is decommissioned. Consumers are informed, dependencies are managed, and the system is safely removed without disrupting the ecosystem.

These phases provide a simple mental model, but the real implementation is more complex. Each phase contains a workflow composed of states and transitions. These workflows vary across organizations and evolve over time. Governance models change, technologies evolve, and organizational structures shift.

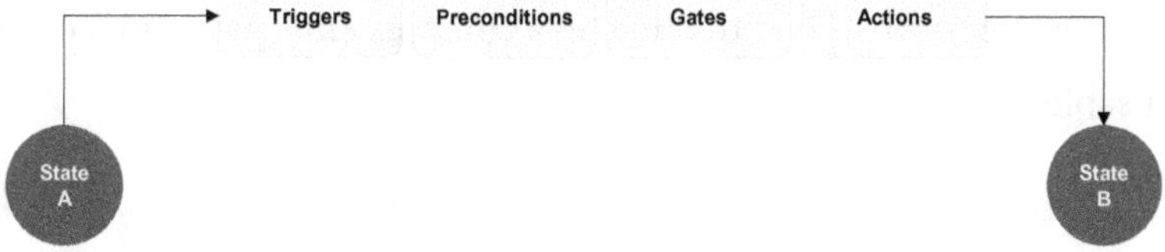

For this reason, the lifecycle cannot be hardcoded. It must be configurable and evolvable by design.

Integrating with the Enterprise Ecosystem

A Data Product is deeply embedded in the enterprise ecosystem, and its lifecycle reflects that.

Architectural reviews involve Enterprise Architecture Management systems. Budget approvals connect to ERP platforms. Dataset registration flows into data catalogs and governance tools. Data modeling integrates with enterprise information modeling systems. Security validations rely on identity providers and access management frameworks. Infrastructure provisioning interacts with cloud platforms, ticketing systems, and DevOps pipelines.

In real-world scenarios, dozens of systems and processes intersect. Each step belongs to a different team and follows a different logic.

Without orchestration, the experience becomes fragmented.

The platform does not replace these systems. It connects and blends them into an ecosystem. It coordinates their interactions, aligns their timing, and presents them as a coherent journey. It acts as the control layer that makes a complex enterprise landscape usable.

From Documentation to Execution

One of the most underestimated problems is how the lifecycle is represented.

When it exists only as documentation, it has limited value. It describes what should happen, but it does not help people act. It does not reduce uncertainty or guide decisions.

When the lifecycle is implemented in the platform, it becomes executable. It guides teams through the process, enforces preconditions, triggers integrations, and surfaces the right information at the right time.

This is the shift from static governance to operational governance.

The Data Product Factory

The Data Product Factory is the capability that helps data product teams **build, evolve, and manage data products across their entire lifecycle**, while remaining compliant with the architectural, governance, security, and compliance principles defined at the platform level. Its primary objective is not control, but **enablement**: reducing the cognitive load associated with all the non-functional responsibilities that inevitably come with building data products at scale.

In a decentralized environment, autonomy is only sustainable if teams are not forced to constantly reason about architecture standards, governance rules, security constraints, and compliance obligations. The Data Product Factory absorbs this complexity on behalf of the teams. It makes it easy to do the right things and deliberately harder to do the wrong ones—without making users' lives miserable or turning the platform into a bureaucratic gatekeeper.

A clear example is metadata production. Metadata is a foundational element for governance, compliance, discovery, and automation. Yet asking teams to manually author complex YAML files—often with unfamiliar syntax and hidden constraints—inevitably leads to frustration, errors, and inconsistency. The factory addresses this by facilitating metadata creation through every possible means: structured user interfaces, guided workflows, validation feedback, and AI-assisted authoring. Metadata becomes a natural by-product of building a data product, not an additional chore imposed after the fact.

Another core responsibility of the Data Product Factory is **architectural alignment**. The factory continuously verifies that data products are being built in line with the target architecture defined for the organization. This includes ensuring teams adopt appropriate data modeling approaches, expose data through the correct protocols, apply consistent orchestration patterns, and implement data quality and reliability mechanisms coherently. These aspects are not optional details. They are what allow the ecosystem to function as a whole.

When autonomy and decentralization are enabled, the platform must still ensure that data products work well **together**, both technically and semantically. Data products built by different teams, in different domains, and potentially by different vendors must still interoperate. At a minimum, it should be possible to combine them easily—for example, joining data products across domains without heroic integration efforts. The factory plays a key role in enforcing the shared conventions that make this possible.

The Data Product Factory is also responsible for guiding teams through the **data product lifecycle**. A data product does not jump directly from an idea to production. It moves through defined stages, such as prototype, draft, quality assurance, production, and retirement. Each stage comes with explicit expectations: technical readiness, metadata completeness, maturity of implementation, and compliance guarantees. These expectations are defined by data product governance and reflected in the operations that are allowed at each stage.

This is where the strong synergy between the Data Product Factory, Data Product Governance, and Data Product Operations becomes evident. Governance defines the rules. Operations enforce them. The factory guides users so that compliance becomes the natural outcome of following the workflow, not an after-the-fact validation that blocks progress.

Reducing effort and cognitive load is particularly critical at the very beginning of a data product's life. Moving from zero to one is often the hardest step. Without guidance, teams face the blank page syndrome, which leads to divergent implementations and erosion of standards. This risk is amplified when teams belong to different business domains, have different technical backgrounds, or rely on different system integrators.

Blueprints and templates are therefore a central element of the Data Product Factory. They provide a concrete, opinionated starting point that encodes best practices and architectural intent. Teams do not start from nothing; they start from a shared foundation. This dramatically reduces variability at the artifact level while still allowing flexibility where it matters.

Finally, the Data Product Factory must be deeply integrated with the **software development lifecycle**, and in particular with Git. Git must remain the source of truth for data products: code, infrastructure definitions, documentation, and metadata all live together and evolve together. This ensures a DevOps-friendly workflow, supports standard branching and versioning models, and allows data products to be managed with the same rigor and discipline as any other software system.

In summary, the Data Product Factory is where intent becomes implementation. It translates architectural principles and governance rules into concrete guidance, tooling, and workflows that teams can actually use. When designed well, it does not feel like control—it feels like leverage.

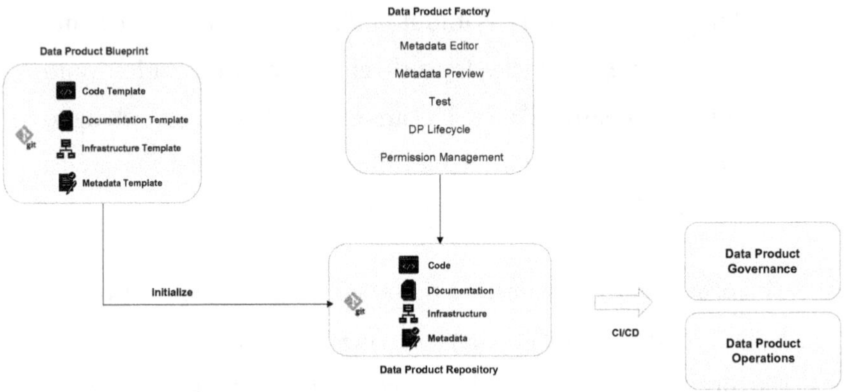

Reducing Cognitive Load for Data Product Teams

One of the least discussed but most decisive factors in building successful platforms is **cognitive load**. We often talk about scalability, governance, and interoperability, but rarely do we stop to ask: How much mental energy does a data product team need just to get started? How hard is it for them to move from idea to implementation? The answers to these questions often determine whether a platform will thrive or be quietly bypassed.

Cognitive load refers to the mental effort required to perform a task. In the world of platform engineering, this has become a central concept. Teams cannot focus effectively on delivering business value if they are constantly burdened by the details of infrastructure, compliance, and tooling. A well-designed platform reduces this load, guiding teams along proven paths and freeing them to concentrate on the one thing only they can do: embedding business knowledge into data products.

But reducing cognitive load is not as straightforward as it sounds. In fact, many well-intentioned attempts to simplify development have had the opposite effect, creating more constraints, tighter coupling, and eventually frustration. Let us explore why.

The Engineer's Temptation: Frameworks that Simplify Everything

Every experienced software engineer, when faced with recurring complexity, feels the same temptation: build a framework.

Frameworks are attractive because they seem to offer a single-stroke solution. Why force every team to reinvent a data pipeline, a logging mechanism, or a security control, when you can build a framework that does it for them? Wrap up best practices, expose a neat API, and let teams build on top of it. At first glance, this feels like the perfect way to reduce cognitive load: hide the complexity, expose only the essentials, and standardize the approach.

I know this temptation well. In my career, I have built dozens of frameworks aimed at simplifying and accelerating the development of data pipelines. Every single one followed the same adoption curve. In the beginning, adoption was enthusiastic.

Teams were delighted that they could deliver known use cases faster, without having to reimplement the basics. For the scenarios foreseen by the framework creators, the tool was a perfect fit.

But then reality intervened. Business requirements evolved. New use cases emerged. Technologies shifted. Suddenly the framework was no longer a perfect fit. It lacked the flexibility for the unexpected. Worse, it introduced a new form of coupling: the change management of the framework team became inseparably tied to the delivery of every team using it.

When a critical business scenario could not be realized within the boundaries of the framework, what happened? The framework flipped from being an enabler to being an obstacle. Teams started looking for workarounds, bypasses, or alternative tools. The framework became hostile.

This pattern is universal.

> *Frameworks solve the first 80% quickly,*
> *but they struggle with the long tail of variability.*

And in data product development, that variability is not a luxury—it is the essence. Every domain has unique needs, every business evolves, and every technology cycle brings new possibilities. The more tightly we bind teams to a framework, the more fragile the entire ecosystem becomes.

The Hidden Risks of SDKs

In software, frameworks are often delivered as SDKs—libraries that teams import directly into their code. This seems harmless at first, but it introduces a time bomb.

Once an SDK is included in hundreds of artifacts across an enterprise, it becomes a **mission-critical dependency**. A single bug, performance issue, or security vulnerability in the SDK ripples across every data product that depends on it. Suddenly, what was meant to simplify delivery has turned into a systemic risk.

Imagine this scenario in the context of data products. An SDK bug prevents pipelines from executing correctly. Overnight, dozens of mission-critical data products fail. Or worse, a vulnerability is discovered in the SDK. Now the entire company is exposed, across every business domain, because one library sits at the heart of them all. The trust painstakingly built in the platform evaporates overnight. This is not hypothetical. The software industry has seen countless examples: critical bugs in shared libraries, zero-day vulnerabilities in common dependencies, supply chain attacks. In a data platform, the blast radius is even larger because data products are inherently transversal. A single SDK becomes the point of failure for the entire enterprise.

For a platform that must serve the entire company, this is unacceptable. There is no space for embedding a development framework or SDK at the core of data product delivery.

An Alternative Path: Templates and Blueprints

So if frameworks and SDKs are traps, what is the alternative? The answer lies in **templates and blueprints**.

A template is not a library. It is a starting point: a piece of source code that can be cloned, customized, and owned by the team building the data product. Instead of forcing every team to start from a blank page, the platform provides ready-made scaffolds that embody best practices, include third-party libraries where needed, and encode standards for interoperability and security.

The difference is subtle but profound. With a template, the platform accelerates the start but does not control the journey. The data product team owns the code from the moment of creation. They can adapt it, extend it, or even replace it entirely. The platform is no longer a dependency in their runtime—it is a coach that gave them a strong starting position.

For example, consider data pipelines. A platform might offer multiple templates: one for Spark-based pipelines, one for dbt, one for Flink streaming. Each reflects best practices for that technology, including logging, error handling, and governance hooks. The data product team chooses the template that fits their needs, and within minutes they have a working pipeline skeleton. They are not forced into a single framework; they are guided toward proven patterns.

This approach dramatically reduces cognitive load. Teams no longer need to design everything from scratch. They do not waste time debating folder structures, connection management, or basic observability. Instead, they inherit a template where these decisions are already made. Their energy is spent where it matters: embedding business logic, modeling data correctly, and delivering value.

The critical step in this model is ownership. After the initial boost, the data product team must own the code of its data product. This disassociates the responsibilities of the platform team and the data product team. The platform team's job is to provide guardrails, templates, and governance; the data product team's job is to implement and maintain their product. This separation protects both sides. The platform team avoids being dragged into the day-to-day evolution of every product, while the product team avoids being blocked by the platform's change cycle. Each evolves at its own pace, connected by contracts and policies, not by shared code dependencies.

A common objection to the template approach is obvious: What prevents a data product team from simply deleting all the template code and diverging completely from standards?

The answer is governance. The platform must include computational policies that enforce non-negotiable aspects of interoperability, security, and quality. Policies can require the presence of certain logging, the use of specific authentication methods, or the definition of metadata. They can check compliance during deployment and block non-conforming artifacts.

At the same time, policies must allow for exceptions. There will always be scenarios where divergence is legitimate—new technologies, special business requirements, or unforeseen use cases. The key is to allow this divergence consciously, not accidentally.

> *A governance system that enforces guardrails but permits exceptions provides both safety and flexibility.*

This balance is impossible to achieve with frameworks, because frameworks force all divergence to happen inside their codebase. Every exception becomes a request to extend the framework, creating bottlenecks and coupling. Templates, by contrast, allow divergence locally, without breaking the global system.

Platform Investment Strategy

Another advantage of the template model is strategic.

Building a framework requires endless investment. Every new use case, every new technology, every new pattern must eventually be supported by the framework team. The backlog never ends, because the framework has to be all things to all people.

Templates, on the other hand, are selective. The platform team can decide where to invest: which templates to create, which technologies to support, and which features to include. Not everything needs a template. In fact, most things will not get one.

The platform team focuses on the highest-value accelerators: the 20% of use cases that cover 80% of needs.

This is a crucial point in product thinking. Building a product is not about adding every possible feature. It is about deciding what **not** to build. Resources are finite. The platform team must focus on what reduces cognitive load most effectively, not on satisfying every edge case. Templates embody this strategy.

Cognitive Load in Practice

Let us consider a concrete example. Imagine a team in the Sales domain is tasked with building a Customer360 data product. Without templates, they face a daunting set of questions:

- How should we structure our repository?
- Which CI/CD pipeline should we use?
- How do we enforce logging standards?
- Which libraries are approved for data quality checks?
- How do we expose observability metrics to the platform?
- How do we declare our data contract?

Each of these requires decisions, research, and alignment with platform standards. The cognitive load is immense before a single line of business logic is written.

Now imagine the same scenario with templates. The team selects the "Customer Data Pipeline (dbt)" template. Within minutes, they have a repository with standard structure, a preconfigured

CI/CD pipeline, logging already integrated, data quality checks embedded, observability endpoints exposed, and a stub data contract defined. Their task is no longer to design the basics; it is to adapt the scaffold to their business logic. The cognitive load is reduced by an order of magnitude.

This is not about dumbing down the process. It is about focusing attention where it matters. The Sales team's expertise is not in designing logging frameworks—it is in understanding customer data. By lowering the cognitive burden of technical scaffolding, the platform frees them to focus on business value.

Lessons from Platform Engineering

This philosophy aligns with what the field of platform engineering has learned over the past decade. Successful platforms are not frameworks forced on developers. They are **products** designed to reduce cognitive load. They do so by:

- Providing paved paths, not golden cages.
- Offering self-service templates, not rigid SDKs.
- Embedding governance invisibly into workflows, not as external policing.
- Balancing freedom with guardrails, not freedom with chaos.

The North Star of platform engineering is not maximum control. It is maximum leverage: enabling teams to deliver faster, safer, and with less mental strain.

The High Cost of Cognitive Overload

Why does this matter so much? Because cognitive overload has real costs.

When teams are overwhelmed by complexity, they make mistakes. Security controls are forgotten. Metadata is skipped. Shortcuts are taken. The result is fragile data products that erode trust.

Worse, cognitive overload drives shadow IT. If the platform is too hard to use, teams will find ways around it. They will build their own pipelines, adopt their own tools, and bypass governance. Once that happens, the platform loses credibility, and adoption collapses.

The opposite is also true. A platform that reduces cognitive load builds loyalty. Teams come back because it saves them time. They trust it because it makes their lives easier. Adoption grows not by mandate but by attraction.

Conclusion: Guardrails, Not Frameworks

Reducing cognitive load is not a side concern. It is the heart of platform adoption.

Frameworks and SDKs seem tempting, but they introduce coupling, systemic risk, and eventual hostility. Templates and blueprints, by contrast, offer acceleration without dependency, guidance without control, and ownership without lock-in. Combined with computational governance, they strike the right balance: reducing cognitive load while preserving autonomy and flexibility.

In the end, the measure of a platform is not how sophisticated its technology is, but how simple it makes life for its users. If a data product team can go from idea to implementation without drowning in complexity, the platform has succeeded. If they can focus on business logic while trusting the scaffolding beneath them, the platform has created real value.

Reducing cognitive load is not just a usability concern. It is a governance strategy, a resilience strategy, and ultimately, the only way to scale data product development across a complex enterprise.

SDLC Integration

A Data Product Management Platform must be fully integrated with the software development lifecycle. This is essential to embrace DevOps principles and to ensure that data products are treated as first-class software artifacts, fully compliant with enterprise policies. Reusing the standard CI/CD pipelines already adopted across the organization is critical, especially those designed to guarantee the production of secure, reliable software.

Preserving familiar DevOps practices lowers the barrier to entry. Software engineers can onboard quickly without being forced to learn bespoke processes or tools, and the broader community experiences less friction. At the same time, these practices help maintain a consistently high level of software quality, which directly contributes to the overall quality and trustworthiness of the data product.

By assimilating a data product to a software artifact and using Git as the primary repository and source of truth for all its components—infrastructure definitions, application code, metadata, and documentation—we obtain a single unit of change management. This allows us to manage data product evolution through a unified lifecycle, rather than inventing a separate, ad hoc process.

In practice, we simply extend the existing software lifecycle to data products.

This approach enables teams to adopt standard branching models to develop new features in parallel, even across different teams and timelines. It becomes straightforward to roll back a data product to a previous version or to patch a production release without accidentally mixing fixes with features still under development. Change becomes controlled, observable, and reversible.

Environment management is equally important. The same version of a data product must be deployable across multiple environments—development, quality assurance, and production—by externalizing configuration and environment-specific variables. This guarantees consistency across stages while preserving the ability to test safely and progressively.

Finally, CI/CD pipelines must integrate tightly with both governance checks and automated deployment procedures. If either governance validation or deployment fails, the pipeline should stop and provide precise, actionable feedback to the user. In this model, CI/CD is not just a delivery mechanism; it becomes the backbone that enforces quality, compliance, and repeatability across the entire data product lifecycle.

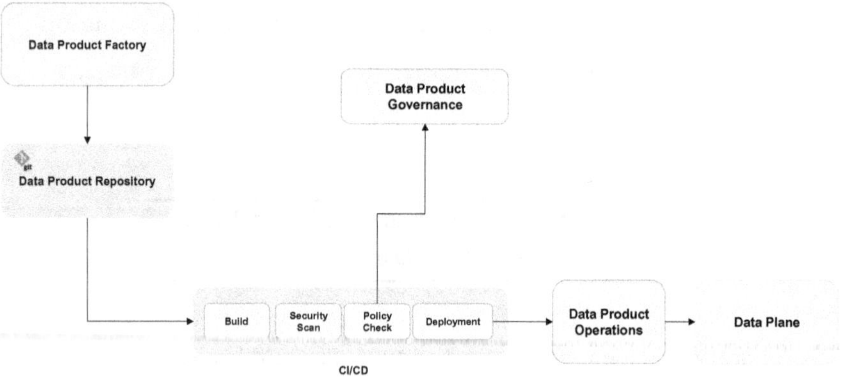

Data Product Operations

One of the most decisive moments in enabling a data product team to reach full autonomy from the platform team is deployment.

Deployment is where all the promises of self-service, decentralization, and ownership are either fulfilled or exposed as wishful thinking. It is the moment when change management stops being an internal concern of a single team and becomes visible to the rest of the organization. A deployment affects consumers, upstream and downstream dependencies, SLAs, and expectations across the ecosystem. From that moment on, the data product is no longer "just code" or "just data": it is a shared asset with real consequences.

True autonomy means being able to perform an end-to-end deployment independently.

No tickets. No handovers. No side-channel coordination with infrastructure or platform teams. It means owning not only the happy path, but also recovery: being able to detect when something goes wrong, understand why, and restore a safe state without external intervention. Finally, it means being able to confidently communicate to the wider community that a deployment has completed successfully and that the promises made by the data product are still valid. If any part of this process requires another team to step in, autonomy is already broken.

What Deployment Really Means for a Data Product

An end-to-end deployment of a data product is rarely a single action, even if it should feel like one. In practice, it involves several distinct responsibilities that must be coordinated coherently. First, the infrastructure required to run the data product must exist. Depending on the adopted blueprint, this may include provisioning storage, configuring network access, allocating compute resources, or setting up runtime environments. Second, the software itself must be deployed: pipelines, transformations, services, schedulers, or any other executable component that implements the data product's logic. Third, metadata must be published: ownership, contracts, documentation, lineage, SLAs—everything that allows the rest of the organization to understand, discover, and trust the product.

All three aspects are inseparable. A data product that runs but is undocumented is not consumable. A data product that is documented but not running is misleading. A data product whose infrastructure exists but whose software is inconsistent is unreliable.

Full autonomy means that a single team can perform all of these steps without dependency on others. At the same time, deployment is inherently complex. That complexity does not disappear just because we want autonomy. It moves.

The responsibility of the platform team is precisely to **absorb that complexity** and expose a radically simpler experience to data product teams. Ideally, deployment should feel like a one-click operation, even if under the hood it triggers dozens of coordinated actions.

Why Infrastructure Automation Alone is Not Enough

Many platforms fail at this exact point. Because platforms are often built by teams with a strong infrastructure background, they tend to equate self-service with infrastructure automation.

Terraform modules are created, pipelines are templated, and documentation explains how teams should glue everything together. On paper, this looks like enablement.

In reality, it is not.

If a data product team has to interact directly with Terraform, Helm charts, or low-level provisioning tools, we are not providing a self-service platform. We are providing a framework. Worse, we are shifting cognitive load rather than reducing it. The team now has to acquire, retain, and debug expertise in tools that are orthogonal to their actual responsibility: delivering value through data.

A genuinely one-click experience cannot involve tickets, but it also cannot require intimate knowledge of infrastructure tooling. Otherwise, autonomy exists only for the few teams that already have strong platform skills, while everyone else remains dependent.

Transparency and Error Handling as Part of Autonomy

Reducing cognitive load does not mean hiding everything.

Autonomy requires **full transparency of operations**. A team performing deployments independently must always know what is happening, which step is currently running, and what state the system is in. When something goes wrong, errors must be understandable, contextualized, and actionable.

Abstracting Terraform but then exposing raw Terraform error messages is a common failure mode. In that situation, teams are forced either to learn Terraform anyway or to open a ticket with the platform team. In both cases, the promise of self-service is broken.

Consistency matters. If the platform shields users from complexity, it must do so end to end, including error semantics, recovery options, and rollback behavior. Autonomy without intelligibility is just delegated frustration.

Deployment is Only One Operation

Deployment is the most visible operation, but it is not the only one that matters.

A data product evolves over time. Teams must be able to release upgrades, introduce changes safely, and eventually retire a product when it no longer provides value. Each of these actions carries risk, and each must be supported with the same design philosophy as deployment.

To act responsibly, teams also need validation and audit capabilities. Before performing an operation, they must understand its potential impact. After performing it, the platform must retain evidence of what happened, when, and why.

In Data Mesh terminology, commands sent to a running data product are often referred to as **control ports**. These commands interact with the internal state of the data product: backing up data, resetting state, restarting schedulers, triggering reprocessing. All these actions are mediated by the platform to ensure consistency, observability, and auditability across the ecosystem.

Operations and control ports belong firmly to the **Control Plane**. Their purpose is not to execute data logic, but to interact with the data plane in a safe, accountable way. When designed correctly, they become the final pillar of autonomy. Teams can act independently, recover quickly, and evolve their products without friction or ambiguity.

Composability and Atomicity

A data product is a system with variable and often unpredictable complexity.

At a high level, a blueprint may describe a data product as a combination of storage, processing logic, and one or more output ports. But real implementations rarely remain that simple. A single data product may include multiple storage layers for different access patterns, several pipelines with distinct responsibilities, sophisticated scheduling logic, and an evolving set of output ports whose number and shape are not known upfront.

Dependencies naturally emerge between these components. Storage must exist before pipelines can write to it. Orchestration logic must come after core components are in place. Output ports often depend on specific transformations or storage layers. These dependencies are not always obvious at design time.

Trying to hardcode all these assumptions into the platform inevitably leads to rigidity. Instead, the platform must rely on a **dynamic orchestrator** that can interpret the data product descriptor and derive a coherent deployment plan. Cardinalities, dependencies, and ordering must be inferred, not predefined. The same logic must apply in reverse during undeployment, ensuring that components are torn down safely without leaving orphaned resources behind.

Atomicity in Production, Composability in Development

Data products are often described as atomic units of deployment—and this is absolutely true in production.

A data product carries SLAs and consumer expectations. Allowing a partially deployed or partially broken data product to reach consumers is unacceptable. For this reason, deployment in production must be atomic: either the entire data product is deployed successfully, or it is not deployed at all.

However, strict atomicity clashes with the iterative nature of software development. In development and testing environments, teams need to work on individual components. A developer must be able to change and test a single pipeline without redeploying the entire data product every time.

This is where **composability** becomes essential.

While working on a single component, dependencies must still be respected. If a pipeline depends on a storage layer, deploying that pipeline must implicitly deploy the required storage as well. The platform must manage this automatically, orchestrating just enough of the system to make iteration possible without overwhelming the developer.

Done well, this approach dramatically improves developer experience and sustainability. Teams can iterate quickly without losing sight of the larger system.

Change Without Disruption

In production environments, atomicity alone is not sufficient. Atomic deployment ensures that a data product is either fully deployed or not deployed at all, but it does not address what happens *when change goes wrong*. For this reason, atomicity must be paired with robust change management strategies whose primary goal is always the same:

> *Enable change without disrupting consumers.*

In the world of data systems, this goal is particularly challenging.

Blue–green deployment is often cited as the ideal strategy. In its pure form, the existing version of a data product continues to serve consumers while a new version is brought up in parallel. Only when the new version is fully operational does traffic shift. In application systems, this pattern is relatively common. In data systems, however, it is only feasible under specific conditions.

Data products are frequently stateful. They rely on persistent storage, historical data, and long-running pipelines. Duplicating the entire runtime state to support a full blue–green setup can be prohibitively expensive, technically complex, or simply impossible. For this reason, blue–green deployment should be seen as a desirable option where conditions allow it, not as a universal assumption.

What must always be available, regardless of the deployment strategy, is **controlled rollback**.

When a new version of a data product is deployed and something goes wrong, for any reason, the platform must be able to restore the previous version quickly and safely. Failures can occur due to code defects, configuration errors, unexpected data characteristics, infrastructure issues, or downstream incompatibilities. The root cause does not matter. What matters is that the platform can return the system to a state where consumer promises are still met.

Rollback is not an afterthought. It is a core capability of responsible change management. Without it, every deployment becomes a high-risk event, and teams will naturally become conservative, slowing down innovation.

Managing Breaking Changes

Change without disruption becomes even more critical when dealing with **breaking changes**.

A breaking change is not simply a failed deployment. It is a deliberate evolution of a data product that invalidates existing consumer assumptions: schema changes, semantic changes, contract changes, or behavioral changes. In these cases, rollback alone is not sufficient, because the new version may be correct and necessary—consumers simply need time to adapt. For this reason, the platform must support the ability to **deploy multiple versions of the same data product concurrently**.

Running two versions side by side allows producers to release a new version while keeping the previous one available. Consumers can migrate at their own pace, update their dependencies, and validate their integrations before switching. During this transition period, both versions are first-class citizens of the platform, each with its own lifecycle state, contracts, and observability signals.

This capability is essential to preserve trust in a decentralized ecosystem. Without it, teams are forced into coordinated releases, ad hoc communication, or artificial freezes—all of which undermine autonomy.

Supporting parallel versions is not about encouraging fragmentation. It is about acknowledging that coordination across teams takes time, and that the platform must absorb that complexity rather than pushing it onto its users.

Undeployment: Tearing Down Safely

Deployment and upgrade are only part of a data product's lifecycle. The platform must also support **undeployment** as a first-class operation.

Undeployment is not simply deleting resources. A data product is composed of multiple interdependent components: storage, pipelines, schedules, output ports, metadata, and contracts. Removing these components must respect dependency order and lifecycle semantics. A safe undeployment process ensures that:

- Dependent systems are identified and warned.
- Consumers are notified in advance.
- Resources are released in the correct order.
- No orphaned infrastructure or metadata is left behind.

Undeployment must be deliberate, observable, and auditable. It is an operation with ecosystem-wide implications, not a local clean-up task.

Retirement: Ending a Data Product Responsibly

Retirement goes one step further.

While undeployment focuses on the technical act of tearing down a data product, **retirement** is a business and governance decision. It marks the formal end of a data product's life.

Retiring a data product means:

- Declaring it no longer supported.
- Preventing new consumers from adopting it.
- Managing a grace period for existing consumers.
- Ensuring that contractual obligations are respected.
- Preserving historical metadata and audit trails.

A retired data product should not disappear silently.

Its existence, ownership, and history remain part of the organizational memory. This is critical for traceability, compliance, and understanding past decisions.

The platform must make retirement explicit, visible, and irreversible once completed. Otherwise, "zombie" data products accumulate, eroding trust in the marketplace and confusing users.

Operations as a Foundation of Trust

Deployment, upgrade, rollback, parallel versioning, undeployment, and retirement are all **Control Plane operations**. They do not execute data logic, but they shape how data products evolve and interact with the ecosystem.

When designed correctly, these operations complete the autonomy loop. Teams can:

- Deploy without coordination.
- Recover without panic.

- Evolve without breaking others.
- Retire without leaving chaos behind.

At the same time, the platform protects the wider community by enforcing computational policies and lifecycle rules consistently. No data product can disrupt the ecosystem through negligence or incomplete change management.

Change without disruption is not about eliminating risk. It is about **containing it**, making it visible, and ensuring that the system remains trustworthy even as it evolves.

Data Product Governance

Protecting the Ecosystem

The platform's objective is inherently dual. On one side, it must automate and simplify the work of individual data product teams. On the other, it must protect the wider community. A single negligent deployment must not trigger a snowball effect that degrades trust across the ecosystem.

For this reason, every operation executed through the platform must be guarded by **computational policies**. A data product that violates architectural, governance, or change management rules cannot be deployed. Likewise, a data product cannot evolve if it breaks established contracts.

Composability enables speed and iteration. Atomicity protects trust and stability.

A well-designed Data Product Management Platform must embrace both—not as opposing forces, but as complementary ones.

Because data products live in the data domain, there is a strong tendency to equate governance with data governance. This assumption is flawed. A data product is not just a package of data; it is a software system that includes infrastructure, application logic, data, and metadata. When we talk about governance and about automating it, the real objective is to control, in other words to govern, a software system that produces data. Data governance is part of the picture, but it is only one dimension of a much broader problem.

Looking at the past, we see massive investments in data governance initiatives that have produced disappointing results. Gartner estimates that around 90% of data governance initiatives fail. This is not due to a lack of tools or effort. It is a consequence of a fundamentally broken model.

Governance Without Control is Not Governance

To govern something means to have control over it throughout its lifecycle and to be able to influence its direction of evolution. Traditional data governance approaches are largely passive. They focus on observing what already exists: scanning data, classifying it, documenting it, and instrumenting it. But by the time these activities take place, the data already exists. Tables have been created. Pipelines have been deployed. Transformations are running in production.

At that point, governance has lost its leverage. There is no real ability to influence outcomes, only to assess them after the fact. This is not governance; it is reporting. It may provide visibility, but it does not provide control.

This is one of the core reasons why traditional data governance fails: it operates too late in the process, when the most important decisions have already been made.

The Illusion of Stewardship

In traditional models, roles such as data stewards are introduced to "own" specific datasets. In reality, these roles usually own metadata, not behavior. They can document meaning, define classifications, and assign quality scores, but they cannot change how data is produced.

The real governors of data are data engineers. By releasing a new version of software, they can change a schema, alter business logic, modify refresh schedules, or introduce breaking changes. They control the system that produces the data, and therefore they control the data itself. Any governance model that ignores this fact is built on a false premise.

You cannot govern outcomes if you do not govern the production process.

The Split-Brain Problem of Traditional Governance

Another structural reason for failure is the separation of change management responsibilities. Data change management is typically handled by engineering teams, using Git, CI/CD, and DevOps practices. Metadata change management is handled by governance teams, using data catalogs and manual workflows.

This creates a split-brain system. Two teams manage different representations of what is supposed to be the same product, using different tools, different processes, and different cadences. Divergence is inevitable.

Over time, metadata drifts away from reality. Documentation becomes outdated. Trust erodes. Consumers stop believing what the catalog says because it no longer reflects what actually runs in production. This disconnect is not accidental; it is a direct consequence of treating data and metadata as separate concerns, rather than as parts of the same system.

A data product is the unit of value, and therefore it must also be the unit of change management. One team must own it end to end. That team may include different skills and roles, but ownership and coordination must be unified.

Governing the System, Not Just the Data

When we talk about data products, governance must be redefined around the system that produces data, not around the data alone. This requires governing the entire production process across multiple dimensions:

- **Architectural governance**, to ensure that data products follow shared blueprints, patterns, and best practices.
- **Infrastructure and security governance**, to guarantee that infrastructure, software, and data meet security and compliance standards.
- **Metadata governance**, to ensure that every data product is documented with meaningful, standardized, and contextual information.
- **Data governance**, to ensure that data behaves as promised and is consistent with its declared contracts.
- **Change management governance**, to ensure that evolution happens responsibly, without breaking downstream consumers.
- **Compliance governance**, to ensure adherence to regulations such as GDPR, DORA, the AI Act, and internal policies.

Only when all these dimensions are addressed together can we claim to be governing the system.

From Passive Observation to Proactive Prevention

The most important shift is from reactive governance to proactive governance. Passive governance detects problems after they happen. Proactive governance prevents them from happening in the first place.

Consider GDPR compliance. A traditional governance approach may detect a violation once personal data has already been retained illegally. At that point, the organization must notify authorities and scramble to fix the issue. The damage is already done.

A proactive approach checks whether the data product implements a data deletion pattern and whether it is scheduled correctly before the product reaches production. If this architectural requirement is missing, the platform can block deployment immediately. The breach never happens.

This is the fundamental difference: governance moves upstream, becomes embedded in delivery, and gains real enforcement power.

Governance as Part of Delivery

Governance cannot sit outside the delivery process. It must be an integral part of it and a shared responsibility of the team building the data product. When governance is automated, enforced at build and deploy time, and integrated with the SDLC, it stops being a bureaucratic checkpoint and starts becoming a safety mechanism.

At that point, governance no longer slows teams down. It protects them. It protects consumers. And it protects the organization from the systemic risks that passive, after-the-fact governance has repeatedly failed to contain.

That is what governance really means in a data product world.

Applying DevOps to Governance

When I look for inspiration to challenge the status quo in the data world, I often turn to software engineering. Software engineering has spent decades dealing with problems of process, ownership, quality—in one word, governance. And this is not accidental.

Software desperately needs governance,
and a data product, at its core, is a software system.

Before the advent of DevOps, the software world suffered from a familiar set of problems. Developers had very limited ownership of the code they produced. Testing was performed ex post by a separate team, often under time pressure. Security issues were widespread because best practices were not applied systematically. Documentation, standards, and architectural discipline were treated as optional, or deferred until the end—if they were addressed at all.

These problems had two main root causes. The first was team organization: responsibilities were fragmented, and accountability was diluted. The second was the subjective interpretation of guidelines and quality standards. Best practices existed, but they lived in documents and presentations, not in the delivery process. Whether they were applied or not depended largely on individual judgment.

The DevOps movement introduced a fundamental shift. It made the *definition of done* objective and verifiable. It enabled best practices and guidelines to be codified. It introduced quality gates directly into the software delivery process. And it reorganized teams in a way that increased ownership, pushing responsibility closer to the people who actually build and change the system.

In the data world, we face the very same governance problems. Necessary metadata is often missing or incomplete. Architectural and compliance best practices are inconsistently applied. Quality and accountability are discovered too late, usually when something breaks or when an audit is looming. The conclusion is straightforward: data products must be treated exactly like software systems, because that is what they are.

This is where the concept of quality gates becomes central. Quality gates are powerful because they are embedded in CI/CD pipelines. CI/CD is unavoidable: it is used at every stage of software development and cannot be bypassed. For this reason, anything that must be enforced consistently—anything that must be verified every time—belongs in CI/CD. When a check fails, the developer receives immediate feedback and can iterate quickly, while the context is still fresh and the cost of change is low.

Security vulnerabilities offer a clear example. A developer starts a project, selects some open-source libraries, and builds software on top of them. Months later, just before the production deadline, a security assessment reveals that those libraries cannot be used due to known vulnerabilities. The developer is forced to replace them, refactor large portions of the codebase, and delay delivery by weeks. Yet those vulnerabilities were present from day one. If vulnerability scanning had been part of the CI/CD pipeline, the issue would have surfaced within hours, not months. The developer would have built the system on the right foundations from the start.

The same dynamic applies to data products. Discovering late that a data contract is incorrect, that a PII data deletion procedure is missing, or that a data product requires an RPO (Recovery Point Objective) strategy because it is classified as critical under DORA can cause substantial rework and delays. These are not minor adjustments; they often require structural changes. By contrast, when a data product team knows from day one what must be implemented and why, the process becomes iterative and smooth. Governance stops being a surprise and starts being a guide.

This approach also eliminates a great deal of frustration: "Why didn't you tell us earlier?" or "How were we supposed to know this was required?"

DevOps showed us that governance works only when it is objective, automated, and embedded in delivery.

Applying DevOps principles to governance is not about adding bureaucracy; it is about making expectations explicit, verifiable, and unavoidable—early enough to make the right thing also the easiest thing to do.

Computational Policies

A computational policy is, by definition, a policy that is verified through code and cannot be bypassed. It represents the foundational building block for automating data governance. Without computational policies, governance remains aspirational—described in documents, interpreted subjectively, and enforced inconsistently. With computational policies, governance becomes executable, objective, and repeatable.

Within a Data Product Management Platform, many types of computational policies can exist and be implemented in multiple ways. What matters is not the specific technology used, but the execution model and the point in the data product lifecycle where the policy applies.

Policies by Lifecycle Timing

The first important distinction is based on *when* a policy is executed within the data product lifecycle.

Deploy-Time Policies

Deploy-time policies are executed during the software lifecycle, typically within CI/CD pipelines, when a branch is merged or when a deployment is triggered. These policies do not inspect data, because data does not yet exist. Instead, they validate *human behavior.*

Deploy time is the last moment when organizations still have full control.

Before deployment, changes are cheap, while after deployment, changes become expensive, risky, and often political. Rollbacks affect consumers, fixes require coordination and incidents trigger escalations.

By enforcing policies at deploy time, the platform intercepts risks before they materialize. It creates a clear contract between teams and the organization: you are free to move fast, as long as you stay within the declared guardrails.

Deploy-time policies also have a powerful cultural effect. They remove ambiguity, because teams know immediately whether something is acceptable or not, with no hidden rules.

This point is critical. Code and metadata are the only artifacts produced by humans in the data product lifecycle. Humans do not produce data directly—except in rare cases such as manual data entry. Deploy-time policies, therefore, focus on verifying whether data product teams have followed the rules previously expressed as guidelines and now codified as computational policies.

These policies can validate a wide range of criteria defined by the governance team. One of the most important areas is metadata verification. Metadata is the engine of automation: everything can be represented as descriptive metadata. Whether that metadata later materializes into infrastructure, scheduling, data contracts, or business semantics, it must first be declared and validated.

Deploy-time policies ensure that required metadata is present, consistent, complete, and aligned with platform standards. They turn implicit expectations into explicit checks. Instead of discovering missing documentation, invalid contracts, or non-compliant configurations weeks later, teams receive immediate feedback while they are still developing the product.

Computational policies consume declarative inputs, such as data product descriptors, data contracts, schemas, metadata, or infrastructure definitions, then evaluate those inputs against a set of rules and produce a deterministic outcome: pass, warn, or block.

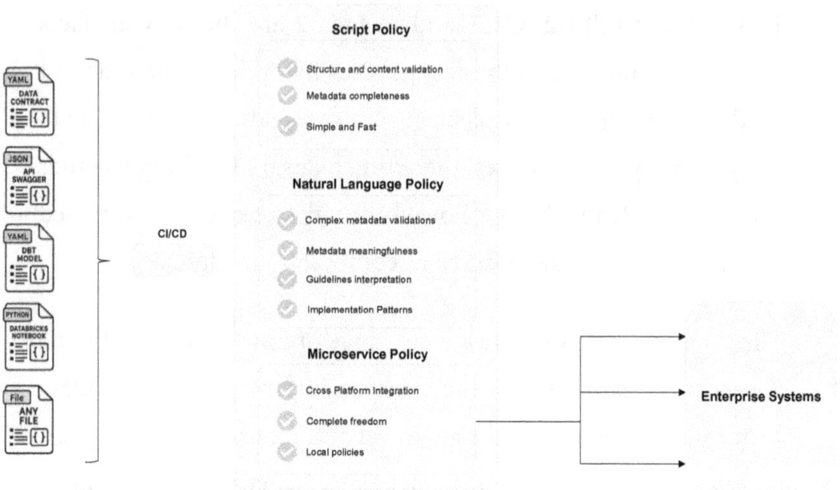

Deploy-time computational policies can be grouped into several broad categories. Each category addresses a different dimension of governance and maturity.

Structural and Descriptor Validation Policies

These are the most basic policies and usually the first ones introduced. Their purpose is to ensure that descriptors, contracts, and definitions are structurally valid and complete. They answer questions such as:

- Is the descriptor syntactically valid?
- Are all mandatory sections present?
- Are required fields populated?

Typical examples include:

- Validating the structure of a data contract YAML.

- Ensuring that ownership, version, and purpose are declared.
- Checking that output ports are defined using supported protocols.

These policies are simple, fast, and non-controversial. They are ideal for early adoption because they introduce governance without friction.

Metadata Completeness Policies

Once the basic structure is in place, organizations quickly realize that *having* metadata is not the same as having *useful* metadata.

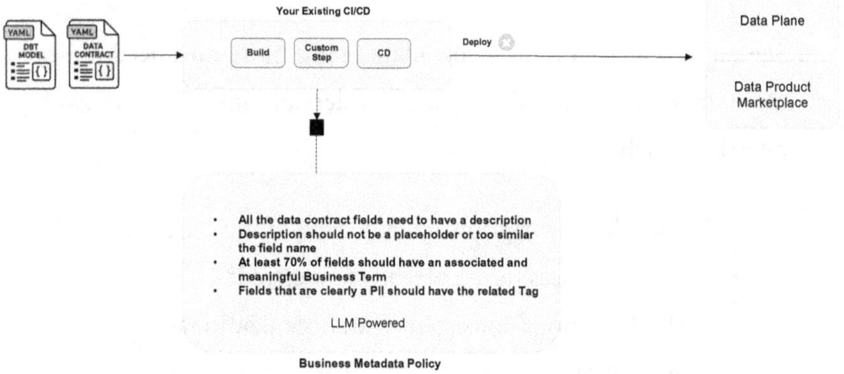

Metadata completeness policies enforce minimum standards around documentation and description quality. They ensure that metadata is not treated as a checkbox exercise. Examples include:

- Every field in a data contract must have a description.

- Descriptions must not be placeholders or identical to field names.
- A minimum percentage of fields must be linked to business terms.

These policies directly support data intelligibility. They force teams to articulate meaning, not just structure. Over time, they dramatically improve the signal-to-noise ratio in catalogs and marketplaces.

Metadata Meaningfulness and Semantic Policies

Completeness alone is not enough. Metadata also needs to make sense.

Semantic policies evaluate metadata using more advanced logic, often involving natural language understanding. They answer questions such as:

- Does this description actually explain the concept?
- Is the business term correctly associated?
- Are definitions consistent with organizational vocabulary?

These policies are particularly powerful when combined with AI-based evaluation. Instead of enforcing rigid templates, they interpret guidelines and patterns.

This is where governance moves beyond static rules and starts encoding organizational knowledge.

Change Management and Breaking Change Policies

Change management is one of the most underestimated sources of risk in data systems.

Breaking change policies compare the version being deployed with the currently active version. They detect incompatible changes and enforce explicit handling.

Typical use cases include:

- Blocking the removal or renaming of fields in a data contract without a version bump.
- Preventing incompatible schema changes on stable output ports.
- Enforcing backward compatibility rules.

These policies protect consumers by design. They also remove emotional friction from change discussions. The platform enforces the rules consistently, regardless of who is deploying.

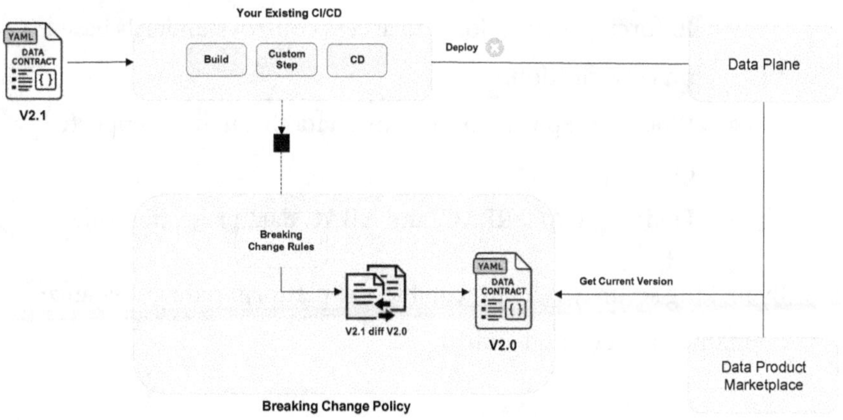

Data Quality and Contract Enforcement Policies

Deploy-time policies can also ensure that quality expectations are defined before data is exposed. Examples include:

- Requiring data quality rules to be declared for critical fields.
- Blocking deployment if quality checks are missing.
- Enforcing minimum coverage of quality rules.

These policies shift the mindset from reactive monitoring to proactive accountability. Quality becomes part of the delivery contract, not an afterthought.

Security and Data Protection Policies

Security and privacy requirements are often documented separately from delivery processes. Deploy-time policies reconnect them. Common examples include:

- Requiring data classification tags to be present.
- Enforcing encryption and access control standards based on classification.
- Blocking exposure of sensitive data through unsupported output ports.
- Defining DAC, RBAC, and ABAC data protection rules.

By making security rules executable, the platform reduces reliance on manual reviews and audits.

Regulatory and Compliance Policies

Regulatory frameworks such as DORA introduce non-negotiable requirements.

Deploy-time compliance policies ensure that regulatory obligations are satisfied *before* systems go live. Examples include:

- Requiring DORA classification for data products.
- Enforcing backup, RTO, and RPO declarations for critical products.
- Ensuring integration with official audit trail mechanisms.

These policies are particularly valuable because they create an auditable, repeatable compliance process that scales across hundreds of teams.

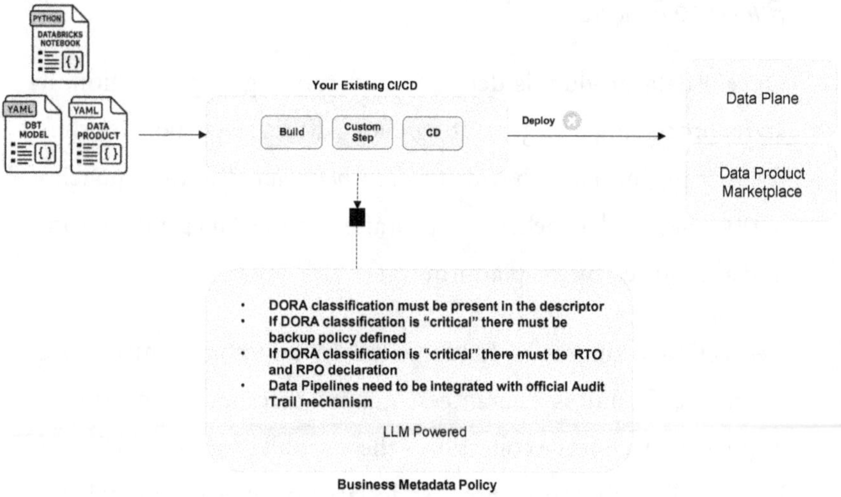

Architecture and Infrastructure Policies

Deploy-time policies can also govern architectural consistency.

Examples include:

- Enforcing approved storage tiers and patterns.
- Validating bronze-silver-gold architectures where required.
- Ensuring that compute components follow supported deployment models.
- Obliging to implement multi-modality on output port protocols (e.g., GraphQL enforcing).

These policies protect the platform from uncontrolled divergence while preserving team autonomy.

Run-Time Policies

Once a data product is deployed and running in production, it starts processing and generating data. At this stage, policies shift focus from human behavior to *data behavior*. Runtime policies verify whether data behaves as promised by the data product team and as required by the platform.

Respecting promises is fundamental in any community. Data contracts, freshness guarantees, quality thresholds, encryption requirements, lineage collection—these are all promises that must be upheld continuously, not just declared once. Runtime policies ensure that what was promised in metadata and contracts is reflected in actual behavior.

Runtime policies often interact directly with data, infrastructure, or processes belonging to a data product. They observe execution, inspect outputs, and detect violations as they happen or shortly after.

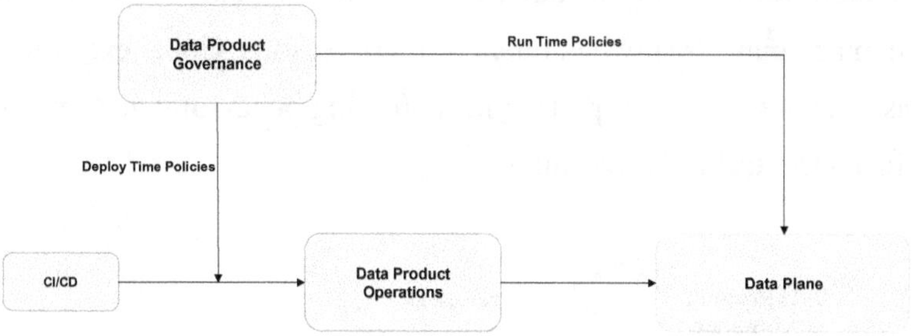

Execution Models: Global vs Local

At runtime, there are two main execution models for computational policies.

Global Execution Policies

A global execution policy runs at the platform level and centrally verifies all data products. These policies typically execute using a platform service principal and therefore require broad permissions to access multiple systems and datasets.

This pattern is familiar: large-scale scans performed by data catalogs or data quality platforms closely resemble global execution policies. While this approach can make sense in certain scenarios, it has significant drawbacks.

Global policies require extensive privileges, increasing security risk. They often lack full visibility into the internal lifecycle of individual data products. Their execution is usually scheduled at arbitrary times, which can delay the detection of violations—sometimes by hours or days. By the time an issue is discovered, damage may already be done. For these reasons, global execution is often a suboptimal pattern for enforcing behavioral guarantees in a decentralized environment.

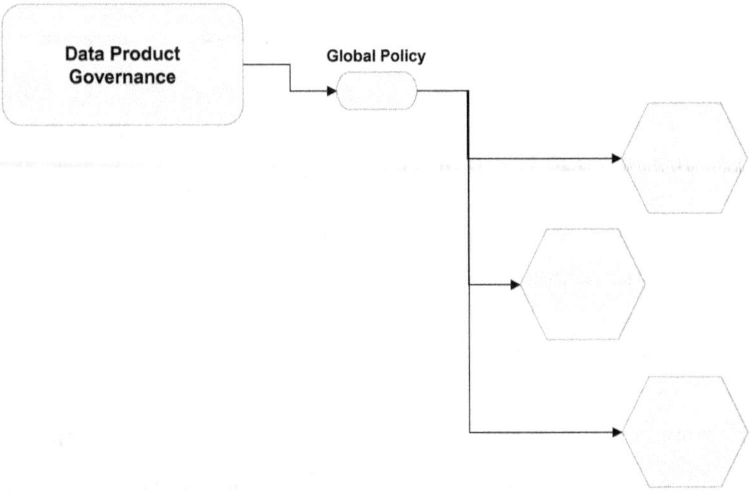

Local Execution Policies

Local execution policies are more complex to implement but far more powerful. In this model, policies execute within the runtime context of the data product itself, using a service principal that belongs to the data product and has access only to its perimeter.

This allows policies to run as part of the data processing flow. When a data product generates new data, a local policy can immediately validate it and detect violations in near real time. Local policies can operate in batch or streaming scenarios and can inspect every record if needed.

Conceptually, local policies can be implemented as logical sidecars to the data processing logic, remaining as close as possible to the execution context. This proximity enables timely enforcement, precise scope, and minimal latency between cause and detection.

There is no universal recipe for implementing local policies. Architectures differ widely: batch pipelines, streaming systems, and scheduled workflows all require different integration patterns. What matters are the principles: locality, timeliness, and clear ownership boundaries.

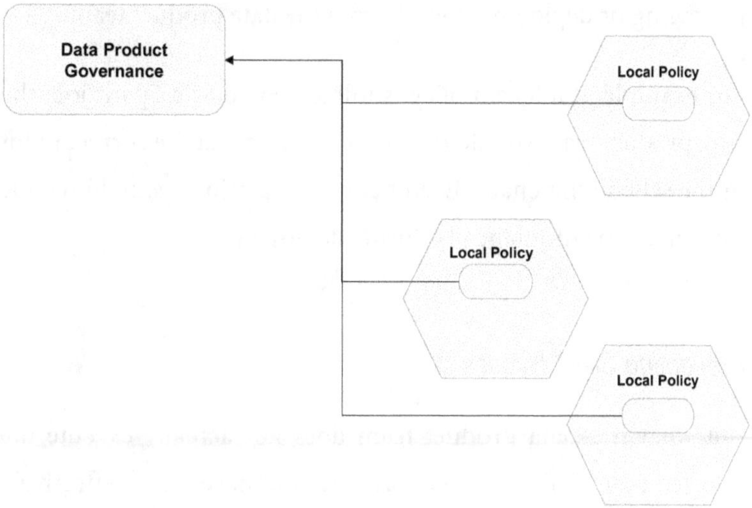

The Role of the Platform

At this point, two questions naturally arise: If policies execute inside data products, what role does the platform play? Does governance become the responsibility of data product teams?

The answer is nuanced. Policies implement platform rules and therefore must not be bypassable, modifiable, or disableable by data product teams. For this reason, the platform team defines and implements policies. The platform team guarantees that policies are correct, consistent, and versioned. Data product teams are responsible only for integration—not for policy logic.

A local policy should be delivered as a separate artifact: a library, a job, or a microservice that can be integrated into the data product architecture with minimal effort. Ideally, the platform itself injects the policy during deployment, without requiring packaging or deployment work from the data product team.

For example, if a local policy is implemented as a Spark job, the data product team should only need to place it at the correct point in the scheduling chain. Even better, the platform should handle this injection automatically during deployment.

Preventing Silent Bypass

But what if a data product team does not actually execute the injected policy? The artifact may exist, but never run—effectively bypassing governance.

The solution is simple and robust. Every local policy should define a minimum execution rate. For instance, a policy may be required to run at least once per week. The platform is aware of this expectation. If a data product fails to emit policy results within the expected timeframe, the platform detects the absence of execution.

The lack of results becomes a signal in itself—a clear indication that the policy is not being integrated or executed. This condition can be treated as a policy violation, triggering the same governance consequences as an explicit failure.

In this way, computational policies close the loop. They are defined centrally, executed locally, monitored globally, and enforced automatically. Governance stops being a set of intentions and becomes an executable system—embedded in delivery, enforced by design, and resilient to human shortcuts.

Observability and Runtime Trust

Trust in data products is not built solely through dashboards.

Metrics are useful, but they are not promises.

What matters at runtime is whether a data product behaves as expected, when it matters.

This is where SLAs stop being numbers and start being commitments.

An SLA is a declaration by the producer: this is what you can rely on. Timeliness, availability, freshness, correctness—these are not abstract qualities. They are guarantees that consumers build upon.

In a network of data products, these guarantees cascade. A downstream product depends on the behavior of upstream ones. Delays propagate. Failures compound. Without visibility into these dependencies, teams operate blind.

Cascading SLAs make this explicit. They allow organizations to reason about end-to-end behavior without centralizing execution. Each data product declares its guarantees. The platform makes dependencies visible. When something breaks, the impact is understood quickly.

Runtime observability, combined with executable contracts, creates a feedback loop. Producers see how their products perform in the real world. Consumers gain confidence that issues will be detected early. Governance shifts from post-mortem analysis to proactive trust management.

Observability is not about surveillance. It is about shared awareness.

The Data Product Marketplace

When we talk about a marketplace in the context of a platform, we refer to the technological infrastructure that enables a real moment of exchange between those who produce data and those who consume it. The true purpose of a platform is to reduce the marginal cost of each individual transaction. This is a core idea in transaction cost theory: value materializes at the moment of transaction, when an exchange actually takes place. Everything else is just potential.

In our case, we are talking about a Data Product Marketplace. The analogy with Amazon is useful. Producers publish their products; consumers search for what they need, understand it, evaluate it, and ultimately buy it. *Buy* is the keyword here. We are not talking about a catalog. We are talking about a marketplace where the transaction actually occurs, the consumer gains access to the good, and can start consuming it.

A marketplace enables disintermediation and removes friction from the exchange of value. One of the fundamental insights of economic theory is that markets scale when intermediaries reduce uncertainty, risk, and transaction costs. What allows a buyer to purchase a product from a complete stranger on Amazon is not trust in the seller, but trust in the platform. The platform guarantees that the exchange happens in a secure, compliant, and predictable way.

Providing this guarantee requires several crucial elements. The first, and perhaps the most important, is product conformity and clarity. Every product on Amazon is described in great detail so that buyers can understand it without physically touching or testing it. The quality of this description matters enormously.

Would you ever buy a product with no photos, or with vague descriptions and missing specifications? High-quality information builds confidence that the product is exactly what the buyer is looking for.

The second element is the guarantee that the product will match what was promised. If the product delivered does not correspond to the description—qualitatively or quantitatively—the buyer can return it. In this case, the platform is taking responsibility for the transaction and protecting the consumer. This guarantee is what incentivizes participation at scale.

Finally, there is the guarantee of delivery: money must reliably translate into shipment. Once again, this is enforced by the platform. If delivery were left to the goodwill of individual sellers—as is often the case in less structured marketplaces like eBay—the willingness to transact would drop significantly.

A Data Product Marketplace must provide the same guarantees:

1. High-quality information describing data products in a clear, standardized, and understandable way.
2. Guarantees that promises are respected, meaning that what the Data Product Owner declares is what actually happens in the data. This is where concepts such as data contracts become fundamental.
3. Guaranteed fulfillment of access requests, so that when a user is authorized, access results in actual consumption

automatically—without waiting for manual, error-prone operations.

These guarantees are typically absent in data catalogs, which is the fundamental difference between the two. A data catalog is designed primarily for technical users focused on governance, troubleshooting, and control. These users need a comprehensive inventory of all data assets in the organization, along with deeply technical information such as lineage, quality metrics, and storage-level details.

A marketplace, instead, targets a very different persona: a consumer-oriented, often business-focused user. This user wants to build dashboards, indicators, models, or even new products. They are interested in understanding what is available, what fits their needs, and how to gain access. In other words, they want to complete a transaction and start creating value. Because the goal is different, the information required is different. A marketplace does not indiscriminately harvest technical metadata. It relies heavily on producer declarations, which must conform to information standards defined by the platform. Moreover, a Data Product Marketplace does not expose the entire inventory of enterprise data assets. That inventory is too large and too noisy to be meaningful for non-technical users. Instead, the marketplace exposes only what can actually be consumed.

This leads to a deeper shift in perspective. The concept of a *data asset*—central to data catalogs—is no longer sufficient to describe value exchange. Value is created when data is consumed. In a data product context, consumption occurs through output ports or, more generally, through *consumable interfaces*.

The same underlying data—say, an Iceberg table—can be consumed through multiple output ports. A data scientist may access it directly at the storage level. A data analyst may query it through a SQL interface. An application may consume the same information via an API or through an event stream derived from the table's changelog. In a marketplace, these are distinct consumption experiences, each with its own contract and guarantees.

Once we adopt this view, talking about "data assets" becomes misleading. Consumable interfaces can be APIs, streams, SQL endpoints, files, or even conversational interfaces. Is a conversational chat powered by data a data asset? Can it be meaningfully represented in a traditional data catalog? What schema would we assign to it?

The difference in user focus and in the goal of enabling real transactions is what truly separates a Data Product Marketplace from a data catalog. A catalog inventories what exists. A marketplace enables exchange. And only where exchange happens does the platform deliver its full value.

Discovery and Shopping Experience

The Data Product Marketplace becomes the point where data is truly democratized, and for this reason, it must be accessible to the entire organization. This simple statement has deep implications. If everyone can access the marketplace, then the experience cannot assume specific technical skills or prior knowledge. There must be no barriers in terms of language, expertise, or accessibility. Everything must be self-explanatory, easy to reach, and easy to understand.

Business users do not think in terms of data products, data assets, or tables. They think in terms of questions, metrics, concepts, and decisions. They search for information using their own language—their domain jargon. If the discovery experience forces them to translate their intent into technical terminology, the marketplace has already failed.

Designing an immersive and effective discovery experience, therefore, depends primarily on the platform's ability to speak the user's language. This is where traditional, technically oriented metadata—often produced by engineers or surfaced by data catalogs—falls short. Technical metadata may be necessary for governance and troubleshooting, but it is largely inadequate as the foundation of a discovery experience aimed at business users.

At an implementation level, discovery must be powered by as much business context as possible. This may take the form of a business glossary, a domain ontology, or a combination of both. These elements are not optional; they are the cornerstone of a usable marketplace.

The platform's responsibility is to ensure that strong, explicit links exist between technical metadata and business metadata, and that these links are maintained over time.

From a user experience perspective, business metadata must take precedence. Discovery should start from business concepts, not from a list of tables. Users should navigate through familiar terms, definitions, and relationships, gradually refining their search until they arrive at consumable interfaces that meet their needs. Tables and low-level data assets should appear only at the final step of a genuinely business-oriented discovery journey.

When discovery is designed this way, the marketplace stops being a technical inventory and becomes a place where people can explore, understand, and trust what the organization has to offer. Only then does democratization move beyond access and become real empowerment.

When we talk about the shopping experience, we are referring to the transaction moment: the act that enables the exchange of value between two parties. In a Data Product Marketplace, this exchange occurs between the data product creator—who has invested time, effort, and resources to build and maintain the data product—and the data consumer, who can extract value from that investment only by accessing and consuming the data.

In this context, the transaction materializes through an access request. This is the equivalent of clicking the "Buy" button in a traditional marketplace. Until that moment, everything else is exploration, evaluation, and intent. The shopping experience begins when a data consumer decides that a specific data product, or one of its consumable interfaces, is what they need to solve a problem or make a decision.

For this transaction to be effective, the marketplace must make the act of requesting access clear, intentional, and simple. The consumer must understand exactly what they are requesting access to, under which conditions, and with which guarantees. This includes clarity on usage constraints, service-level commitments, ownership, and any obligations that come with consumption. Ambiguity at this stage undermines trust and discourages adoption.

At the same time, the shopping experience must respect the investment made by the data product creator. Granting access is not a purely technical operation; it is an accountability decision. The creator is implicitly committing to support, maintain, and honor the promises associated with the data product. For this reason, the platform must support appropriate approval workflows, policy checks, and ownership controls, ensuring that access is granted only when conditions are met.

Once authorization is given, the transaction must complete automatically. Access should translate into actual consumption without manual intervention, tickets, or delays. Permissions must be applied, credentials or endpoints must be exposed, and consumers must be notified. If the marketplace requires human follow-up to finalize access, the transaction remains incomplete, and the value exchange is broken.

A good shopping experience also preserves traceability. Every transaction should be recorded: who requested access, who approved it, when it happened, and under which version of the data product and its contracts. This traceability protects both sides of the exchange and provides the foundation for accountability, auditability, and continuous improvement.

Ultimately, the shopping experience is where the marketplace proves its worth. It turns discovery into action and intent into value. When access is easy, transparent, and reliable, data products stop being abstract assets and become tangible building blocks that teams can confidently rely on to create impact.

Democratization

Democratization is often misunderstood as "giving access to everyone". In reality, democratization means making value accessible, not simply opening doors. A Data Product Marketplace democratizes data when it allows people across the organization to find, understand, and consume data products without requiring deep technical expertise or constant mediation by specialists.

This is why democratization cannot be separated from discovery and shopping. Discovery enables people to orient themselves using their own language and mental models. Shopping enables them to act on that understanding and obtain access. Together, they turn data from an abstract, centralized resource into something people can actively use to solve problems.

True democratization also requires asymmetry to be handled correctly. Not everyone needs the same level of detail, control, or responsibility. Business users should not be forced to reason about tables, pipelines, or storage formats. At the same time, technical users must not lose the ability to inspect, validate, and reason deeply about what they consume. The marketplace must therefore expose varying levels of understanding for the same products, without fragmenting the experience.

Crucially, democratization does not weaken governance—it strengthens it. When consumption happens through a marketplace, access paths are explicit, auditable, and standardized. Visible transactions replace Shadow access, informal data sharing, and undocumented dependencies. In this sense, democratization is not the opposite of control; it is a more scalable form of it.

A marketplace that successfully democratizes data shifts the conversation within the organization. Instead of asking "Who owns this table?" or "Can someone extract this dataset for me?", people start asking "Which data product solves my problem?" That is the moment when data becomes a shared organizational capability rather than a specialist asset.

Data Monetization

Once a Data Product Marketplace is established internally, extending it beyond organizational boundaries becomes a natural evolution. External sharing and data monetization are not separate problems; they are extensions of the same mechanisms that enable internal exchange of value.

> *From a structural perspective, sharing data externally is not fundamentally different from sharing it internally.*

The same guarantees are required: clear product descriptions, enforceable contracts, controlled access, and reliable fulfillment. The main difference lies in the strength of the guarantees and the risk profile. When consumers are external, tolerance for ambiguity drops to zero, and expectations around stability, compliance, and accountability increase dramatically.

A marketplace-based approach makes this extension possible because it already treats data as a product and access as a transaction. External consumers interact with consumable interfaces, not raw assets. Contracts are explicit. Versions are managed. Change management is enforced. This is exactly what is required to turn data into something that can be shared—or sold—safely.

Data monetization does not necessarily mean selling raw data. More often, value lies in *access to capabilities*: curated datasets, enriched views, analytical outputs, APIs, or event streams. A marketplace allows these offerings to be packaged, versioned, and exposed in a controlled way, with clear ownership and traceability. Pricing models, usage limits, and entitlement rules can be layered on top without changing the underlying paradigm.

Perhaps most importantly, external sharing forces rigor internally. The moment an organization considers exposing data products outside its boundaries, all the weaknesses of informal practices become visible. Inconsistent metadata, undocumented behavior, fragile pipelines, and unclear ownership are no longer acceptable. In this sense, data monetization is not just a revenue opportunity; it is a forcing function that drives maturity.

A Data Product Marketplace provides the foundation for this evolution. It creates a continuum from internal democratization to external value exchange, using the same concepts, controls, and operating model. When designed this way, external sharing is not a leap into the unknown—it is simply the next transaction.

The Integration Layer

Integration has always been one of the most challenging areas in IT. For many architects, the word itself is enough to conjure memories of complexity spiraling out of control: endless middleware projects, fragile connectors breaking at the worst possible moment, integration layers that grew into black boxes nobody fully understood. Over the decades, entire generations of tools and methods have promised to "finally solve integration." And yet, the challenge persists.

Why does integration feel so hard? The answer lies in its nature: it is the space between systems. Inside a system, things can be controlled. We can pick the technology stack, enforce patterns, and keep the complexity bounded. But as soon as two systems need to interact, we face all the mismatches: different technologies, different data formats, different performance characteristics, and above all, different ownership.

Integration is where boundaries collide.

For a Data Product Management Platform, this challenge becomes even sharper. We insist on separating the **Control Plane** from the **data plane**. This is non-negotiable: the platform governs, coordinates, and enforces; the data technologies execute, process, and deliver. Mixing the two leads to lock-in and fragility. But if they are separated, they must still talk to each other. The integration layer is the bridge.

A Brief History of Integration

It is useful to step back and look at how integration has been approached in the past. Each generation of technology has left behind patterns that still influence how we think today.

In the earliest days of enterprise IT, integration was literally physical: files transferred overnight from one mainframe to another. These "file drops" were simple and visible—a flat file would appear in a shared directory, signaling that the upstream process had completed. Many organizations still run critical processes on this model, decades later. Simplicity was its strength, but also its weakness: no guarantees on timeliness, no validation of content, and no way to react if the upstream failed.

Then came database-level integration. If two applications shared the same database, integration was "automatic": one would insert a record, the other would read it. Triggers and stored procedures allowed some degree of reactive behavior. This was efficient, but it created dangerous coupling. Changing the schema in one application could silently break another, and soon the database became a hidden web of dependencies.

In the 1990s, middleware promised salvation. Enterprise Service Buses (ESBs) were introduced as central hubs that mediate all interactions. They offered transformation, routing, protocol conversion—in theory, a clean separation between systems. In practice, many ESBs became bottlenecks. All logic flowed through them, governance teams guarded them, and they quickly turned into single points of failure.

The rise of the web brought APIs to the forefront. REST APIs, in particular, democratized integration. Suddenly, any system could expose a stable, documented interface accessible over HTTP. Coupled with the idea of semantic versioning, APIs became contracts that could evolve without breaking consumers. This shift decentralized integration: rather than one giant bus, each system could speak for itself, while consumers had the freedom to pick and choose.

More recently, event-driven patterns have gained traction. Instead of polling or chaining systems in a brittle sequence, producers publish events to a bus, and consumers subscribe to those they care about. This decoupling has proven powerful in distributed architectures, but it comes with its own challenges: defining event schemas, ensuring consistency, and managing at-least-once delivery without duplication.

Why Integration Matters in Data Product Management Platforms

In the world of data product management, integration is not an optional afterthought. It is fundamental to achieving the platform's purpose. Why? Because the platform does not move or process data itself. It governs lifecycles, metadata, policies, and contracts. The heavy lifting of data—pipelines, queries, transformations—happens in the data plane: Databricks, BigQuery, Snowflake, Spark, dbt, Soda, Monte Carlo, or whatever mix the organization has adopted.

This means the platform must integrate at multiple levels:

- **Control Plane to data plane**: The platform declares what a Data Product is, validates descriptors, enforces policies, and triggers deployments—but the actual code runs elsewhere. The two planes need a well-defined handshake.

- **Integration with the software delivery lifecycle (SDLC)**: The platform must connect with CI/CD pipelines, version control systems, and release management processes, so that data product development aligns with established engineering practices.
- **Change management**: Whenever a data product evolves, stakeholders must be informed. Breaking changes must be flagged, deprecations announced, and upgrades coordinated. Integration with change management systems is key.
- **Ancillary tools**: Monitoring dashboards, cost allocation systems, data catalogs, identity providers, notification engines—all of these orbit the platform, and all require integration.

Without a strong integration layer, the platform risks two extremes. At one end, it becomes too isolated: a beautiful conceptual model that nobody uses, because it never connects with reality. At the other end, it becomes too entangled: directly embedded into runtimes, taking on mission-critical execution, and becoming a fragile single point of failure. The art is in finding the balance.

API-First Integration

The most robust pattern for this balance is **API-first integration**.

An API (Application Programming Interface) is not just a technical artifact; it is a contract. It declares what a system offers, under what conditions, and what a consumer can expect in return. If designed with care, APIs are stable enough to decouple systems but flexible enough to evolve over time. Semantic versioning ensures that consumers know whether a new version introduces breaking changes or just enhancements.

In a Data Product Management Platform, every major interaction should be API-based:

- Triggering a deployment of a data product.
- Validating a descriptor against governance rules.
- Querying observability metrics for compliance.
- Requesting access approval workflows.
- Receiving notifications of a contract breach.

This contract-first mindset creates clarity. The platform does not need to know the inner workings of Databricks or dbt; it just needs them to expose an API for what matters. Likewise, when notifying external systems, the platform does not hardcode connections; it sends an API call or publishes a webhook, and the other side decides how to handle it.

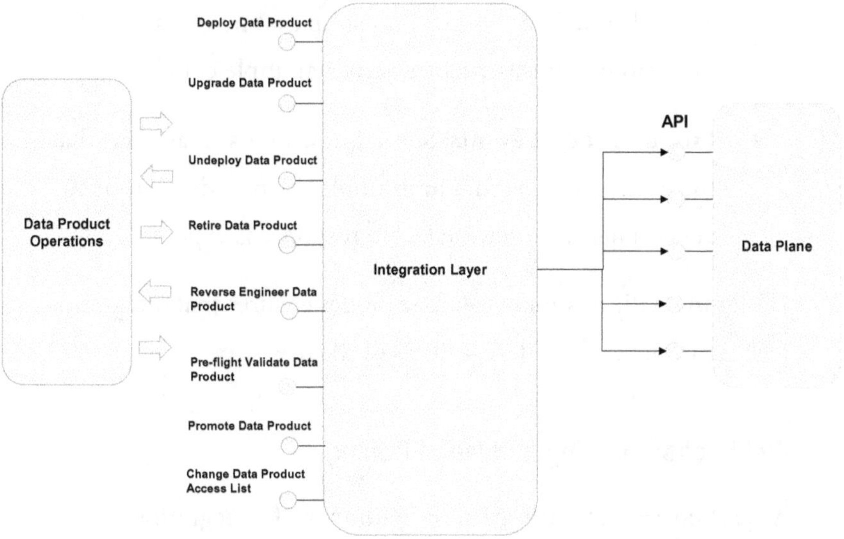

Patterns of API Interaction

Not all interactions look the same. The integration layer must support a spectrum of patterns.

- **Synchronous request–response**: The classic model, where a client asks a question and expects an answer immediately. For example, "Does this descriptor comply with the current policies?"
- **Asynchronous request**: The client makes a call without blocking, expecting the result later. For example, triggering a deployment that may take hours.
- **Long-running jobs with callbacks**: Some processes span hours or days, and consumers need status updates. An

example is a data product bootstrap that involves provisioning infrastructure across multiple clouds.

- **Fire-and-forget events**: Sometimes, all that matters is that the event is delivered. For example, "A new data product version has been released." No response is expected.

Designing APIs to support all four modes ensures that integration feels natural, not forced, regardless of the use case.

Webhooks: Pushing Instead of Polling

A particularly elegant pattern within API integration is the **webhook**. Traditionally, systems that wanted to know about changes had to poll repeatedly: "Has anything changed yet?" This wastes resources and creates lag. Webhooks reverse the model: when an event occurs, the platform notifies subscribers instantly.

Imagine a data product team releases version 2.0 of their "Customer360" product. A webhook can notify downstream consumers that a new version is available. Observability dashboards can subscribe to receive breach notifications in real time. Governance teams can receive alerts when a sensitive attribute is added.

Webhooks transform integration from passive to proactive. Instead of consumers discovering problems after the fact, they are told immediately and can react accordingly. In a decentralized ecosystem, this is vital: no single team can monitor everything, but every team can subscribe to what matters to them.

Benefits of an API-Centric Integration Layer

Why insist so much on APIs and webhooks? Because they bring a set of benefits that align perfectly with the goals of the platform:

- **Decoupling**: Systems evolve independently. As long as they respect the interface, they can change internally without breaking others.
- **Clear segregation of duties**: The Control Plane enforces governance; the data plane executes pipelines. APIs are the handshake, not the glue.
- **Security as a first-class concern**: APIs allow fine-grained authentication, authorization, and auditing. Every interaction can be logged and traced.
- **Future-proofing**: New technologies can be integrated without rewriting the platform by simply adding or extending APIs.

Without this approach, integration becomes brittle, and every new technology threatens to destabilize the whole platform. With it, we can evolve safely.

Why Not Terraform as the Primary Interface?

Terraform's strengths are genuine. Most infrastructure teams already know it. Plan/apply cycles make changes predictable and auditable. The provider ecosystem is mature and covers virtually every cloud resource. For provisioning static infrastructure—

resource groups, networks, storage accounts, IAM bindings—Terraform is an excellent tool. None of what follows disputes that.

The question, as with the operator pattern, is whether Terraform should serve as the primary interface for CI/CD pipelines and data product teams to interact with the platform. The answer is no. Terraform can absolutely live behind an API for specific operations where it makes sense. But exposing it directly as the integration surface creates problems that compound as the platform scales.

The first problem is the ownership model. When Terraform takes control of a resource, it assumes full ownership of its state. From that point on, the resource is expected to be managed exclusively through Terraform. Any external interaction risks creating state drift. This assumption works for static infrastructure components—a resource group, a network, a storage bucket. It breaks down when we deal with richer, behavior-oriented components that evolve across multiple channels over time.

Take a table. Creating or destroying it is only a small part of its lifecycle. Over time, the schema needs to evolve incrementally. Triggers get added. Data masking rules change. Access control policies are refined as new consumers appear. These are not edge cases; they are normal operational activities in the life of a data product. Terraform is not suited to model or manage these evolutions in a granular, expressive, and safe way. Forcing them into Terraform leads to brittle solutions and workarounds. Teams end up stepping outside Terraform for the complex cases—

creating manual steps, breaking automation, or overloading it with responsibilities it was never designed to handle. Either way, cognitive load increases and ownership blurs.

The second problem is the level of abstraction. Terraform understands resources, not intent. It does not reason about deployment phases, dependencies between logical components, lifecycle transitions, or change management semantics. These concepts are central to data product operations. A CI/CD pipeline that calls Terraform directly inherits these limitations: it must encode lifecycle logic, dependency ordering, rollback strategies, and error handling into HCL or wrapper scripts. The platform's intelligence leaks into pipeline configuration, and what should be a platform responsibility becomes a team responsibility.

The third problem, consistent with the argument made for the operator pattern, is feedback and directionality. Terraform's plan/apply cycle is fundamentally one-directional: it pushes declared state onto infrastructure. But data product operations require bidirectional communication. Reverse engineering requires the platform to inspect existing assets—tables, topics, and permissions created outside the platform—and pull information back. Monitoring requires the data plane to push signals to the Control Plane. Undeployment requires dependency checking and negotiation before acting. A Terraform apply cannot do any of this. It provisions forward; it does not negotiate, inspect, or report back in a structured way.

The principle is the same one established earlier in this chapter: the primary interface must be an API. Behind that API, the implementation can vary by operation. Some operations—provisioning a cloud storage account, creating a network policy, setting up an IAM binding—may well delegate to Terraform internally, because Terraform fits those cases well. Other operations—schema evolution, access negotiation, reverse engineering, lifecycle transitions—will use different mechanisms entirely: managed-service SDKs, direct API calls, or custom logic.

This separation keeps Terraform where it adds value without forcing the entire platform into its execution model. The CI/CD pipeline calls the platform's API. The platform decides how to execute each operation. Teams see a consistent, feedback-rich interface. Terraform, where it is used, remains an internal implementation detail—invisible to the user, replaceable without disruption.

Why Not Use the Operator Pattern as the Primary Interface?

The operator pattern has proven its value in managing stateful infrastructure on Kubernetes. Projects like Strimzi for Kafka, the Spark Operator, and the Flink Operator demonstrate that encoding operational knowledge into controllers—upgrades, failover, scaling—is a sound approach when the platform itself is the runtime. The pattern works well in that context, and nothing in this discussion dismisses its usefulness there.

The question is different: Should the operator pattern serve as the primary integration model for a data product management platform? The answer is no, and the reasons are structural rather than ideological.

The first problem is feedback. In an operator-based model, the user declares a desired state and the controller attempts to reconcile reality with that declaration. If reconciliation succeeds, the resource converges silently. If it fails, the failure is often equally silent—or at best, surfaced as a status condition buried in the resource's metadata. The user who triggered the operation receives no direct, structured feedback. There is no synchronous response saying "this failed because the schema violates policy X." There is no callback when a long-running provisioning step completes. There is no error message translated into the language of data products. The user is left polling, inspecting controller logs, or simply waiting, uncertain whether something went wrong or is still in progress.

This matters because data product operations are not fire-and-forget infrastructure provisioning. They are intentional actions performed by people who need to understand outcomes immediately. A deployment that fails a governance check should tell the team exactly which policy was violated and why. An undeployment that cannot proceed because downstream consumers still depend on the product should explain the dependency, not silently retry until a timeout expires. The feedback loop is not a nice-to-have; it is the mechanism through which teams learn, correct, and build trust in the platform.

The second problem is directionality. The operator pattern is inherently one-way: from desired state to reality. The controller watches the declared spec and pushes the world towards it. But data product operations are fundamentally bidirectional. Reverse engineering requires the platform to inspect existing assets in a runtime environment—tables, topics, and permissions created outside the platform—and pull that information back into the Control Plane. Monitoring requires the data plane to push signals back to the platform: SLA breaches, quality failures, and resource consumption. Undeployment requires negotiation, not just deletion: the platform must check consumer dependencies, evaluate impact, and report results before acting. None of these interactions fit naturally into a reconciliation loop. They require request-response semantics, callbacks, event streams, and structured error reporting—exactly the interaction patterns that APIs provide.

This does not mean operators have no place in the architecture. They can absolutely serve as the internal implementation behind an API. When the platform exposes an API for deploying a data product, the service behind that API may well delegate infrastructure provisioning to a Kubernetes operator, use Terraform to provision cloud resources, or call a managed service API directly. The key distinction is between the primary interface and the internal implementation. The primary interface—what the platform exposes to teams, CI/CD pipelines, governance checks, and the marketplace—must be an API. It must support synchronous and asynchronous interaction modes. It must provide structured, actionable feedback. It must enable bidirectional communication. What happens behind that API is an implementation detail that can vary by technology, by environment, and by operation type.

This separation has a practical consequence: the platform can use operators where they add value—managing a self-hosted Kafka cluster, for instance—while using entirely different mechanisms for other operations, without ever exposing that heterogeneity to the user. The user sees one consistent interface. The platform absorbs the complexity of choosing the right execution pattern for each operation.

In short, the operator pattern is a valid execution strategy, not a valid integration model. Elevating it to the primary interface forces a one-way, feedback-poor interaction model onto operations that demand direct communication, structured responses, and bidirectional data flow. APIs provide all of this. Operators, Terraform, managed-service SDKs, and any other execution mechanism can live behind them.

Microservice Architecture

A microservices-based approach is particularly effective for managing data product operations because it aligns naturally with the heterogeneity, variability, and evolution of data products. Data product operations are not uniform tasks; they span deployment, undeployment, partial deployment, reverse engineering, permission management, metadata updates, and many other actions that differ widely in scope, duration, and execution semantics. A microservices architecture provides the flexibility required to handle this diversity without forcing everything into a single operational model.

Microservices can be stateless or stateful, depending on the nature of the operation. Some actions require immediate, synchronous feedback to the user—such as validating a descriptor or checking policy compliance—while others are inherently asynchronous, long-running, or event-driven, such as provisioning resources, migrating data, or propagating permissions across systems. Microservices can support both push and pull interaction models, making them suitable for everything from user-triggered deployments to background reconciliation or discovery processes. This flexibility allows the platform to model operations as they actually are, rather than bending them to fit a rigid execution pattern.

From a software engineering perspective, microservices enable clean separation of concerns and reuse of business logic.

Common behaviors, such as dependency resolution, policy evaluation, audit logging, or error normalization, can be shared across services without coupling them to specific technologies. More importantly, microservices are largely neutral with respect to what they operate on. They do not carry an inherent bias toward infrastructure-level constructs or application-level runtimes. This makes them a strong compromise for managing heterogeneous elements—tables, topics, APIs, permissions, metadata, contracts—through a single, consistent integration model. This is where the contrast with other patterns becomes clear. In the comparison shown earlier, the "pure software" approach maps naturally to a microservices architecture, while "delegation" aligns with the operator pattern. Operators assume continuous reconciliation and tight coupling to runtime state, which may be appropriate in certain infrastructure-heavy scenarios but often becomes overkill in modern, managed data platforms. Microservices, instead, operate at the level of intent and operation: they execute well-defined actions, respect explicit lifecycle transitions, and then get out of the way.

By adopting microservices for data product operations, the platform gains composability, extensibility, and clarity. New operation types can be introduced without rewriting the core. Existing operations can evolve independently. Integration remains uniform even as underlying technologies change. In practice, this results in a platform that is easier to reason about, cheaper to operate, and better aligned with the real operational needs of data product teams—without inheriting the complexity and costs of continuous reconciliation patterns where they are not justified.

Capabilities

To support real autonomy and safe evolution, a Data Product Management Platform must expose a clear and complete set of operational capabilities. These capabilities define how a data product is created, evolved, and eventually removed, and they form the operational contract between the platform and the data product teams. Each operation must be explicit, auditable, and governed, so that change remains intentional rather than accidental.

Deployment is the foundational capability. It represents the act of bringing a data product to life by provisioning required resources, releasing software components, and publishing metadata in a consistent, atomic manner. Partial deployment complements this by allowing teams to deploy or update a subset of components—typically in development or quality environments—while still respecting dependencies and governance rules. This capability is essential to support iterative development without forcing teams to redeploy the entire product every time.

Undeployment is the symmetric operation to deployment. It ensures that a data product or specific components of it can be safely removed without leaving orphaned resources or breaking the assumptions of other products. Retirement builds on undeployment by formalizing the end of a data product's lifecycle. A retired product is no longer active or discoverable for new consumers, while still preserving historical metadata, lineage, and audit information for compliance and traceability.

Reverse engineering is a critical capability in real organizations, where not everything starts from a clean slate. It allows the platform to inspect existing assets—such as tables, topics, or APIs created outside the platform—and reconstruct a data product descriptor from them. This enables teams to bring legacy or experimental work back under governance without forcing disruptive rewrites.

Versioning capabilities govern how data products evolve over time. Minor or patch versions support backward-compatible changes: bug fixes, performance improvements, metadata enrichment, or non-breaking extensions. These versions allow teams to improve products safely without impacting existing consumers. Major versions, on the other hand, represent intentional breaking changes. They introduce new contracts or behaviors and require explicit change management, consumer awareness, and often coexistence with previous versions during a transition period.

Together, these operational capabilities define a complete and coherent lifecycle for data products. They give teams the freedom to iterate and evolve, while giving the platform the tools to enforce stability, accountability, and trust across the ecosystem.

Integration in Practice

Let's make this concrete. Consider a scenario where a new data product is being deployed:

- The data product team commits a descriptor to Git.
- The CI/CD pipeline validates it by calling the platform's API to verify compliance with governance policies.

- The platform responds synchronously with a list of issues, if any.
- If validation passes, the pipeline calls another API to trigger deployment.
- The deployment itself is long-running: infrastructure must be provisioned, jobs created, and access rules applied. The platform responds asynchronously, with a callback once the process completes.
- Once live, a webhook notifies the marketplace that a new version is available. Consumers who subscribe to that product receive the notification instantly.
- At runtime, if the data product fails an SLA, a webhook notifies downstream consumers so they can decide whether to continue or pause.

All of this happens without the platform ever executing a pipeline or serving data. The Control Plane stays in its lane, and the integration layer ensures the handshake.

The Complexity of Data Applications

Why is this especially important in data contexts? Because data applications are inherently more complex than software applications.

A typical software application runs on a runtime like Kubernetes. You package it in a container, deploy it, and the environment is relatively homogeneous. A data application, by contrast, often spans multiple technologies. Part of it may run in Databricks, part in Fabric, part in a specialized tool like Soda for quality checks, and another in Monte Carlo for observability. Each of these technologies has its own runtime, APIs, and quirks.

This heterogeneity means abstraction is limited. We cannot simply pretend they are all the same. Instead, the integration layer must embrace diversity, offering a common set of patterns—APIs, webhooks, contracts—that allow them to interoperate without forcing them into a single box.

Governance Through Integration

Integration is not just about plumbing; it is also about governance. Policies, contracts, and compliance checks must be enforced across the ecosystem. This requires integration. For example:

- At deploy time, the platform checks whether the data product descriptor includes all required metadata.
- At runtime, observability tools report contract breaches back to the platform via APIs.
- Notifications of breaches are pushed via webhooks to consumers and governance teams.

In this way, governance becomes computational—enforced automatically, not manually. Integration is the mechanism that makes this possible.

Lessons from the Past

If history teaches us anything, it is that integration patterns must be designed with humility. Many past efforts failed because they tried to solve too much centrally. ESBs promised to handle every transformation, every protocol, every routing decision—and became choke points. Triggers in databases promised automatic synchronization—and became hidden dependencies. File drops promised simplicity—and became swamps of duplication.

The lesson is clear: keep the platform focused.

Provide APIs and webhooks as contracts. Enforce governance and lifecycles. But let the runtimes execute. Respect the separation of planes. Integration should enable autonomy, not centralize control.

Conclusion: Integration as the Platform's Spine

The integration layer is not a detail to be delegated. It is the spine of the platform. Without it, the separation between Control Plane and data plane collapses, and we fall back into lock-in and fragility. With it, we enable governed autonomy: teams choose the right technologies, but the platform ensures consistency, accountability, and safety.

Integration is the silent enabler. Done well, it disappears into the background, leaving teams free to innovate. Done poorly, it becomes the first source of friction, the reason people bypass the platform, and the root of shadow IT.

This is why, in designing a Data Product Management Platform, we must treat integration not as plumbing, but as architecture. It is the language of collaboration between planes, between teams, between technologies. It is the guarantee that decentralization will not descend into chaos and that governance will not become a bottleneck. It is, in short, the backbone that makes the entire system hold together.

Data Product Observability

Trust is fragile. A Data Product can be carefully designed, thoroughly governed, and correctly deployed, yet still fail its consumers in production. Pipelines can drift. Upstream schemas can change silently. Quality thresholds can degrade over time. SLAs can be missed not because no one cares, but because no one can see what is happening. This is the problem that observability in the Control Plane exists to solve. It is the mechanism through which the platform learns, in real time, whether the promises made by Data Products are being kept.

Why Observability is Not the Same as Monitoring

Monitoring and observability are often used interchangeably, but they address different questions. Monitoring tells you that something has gone wrong: a pipeline failed, a dataset is late, a quality check returned an error. Observability tells you why. It gives you the ability to reason about the internal state of a system from the signals it produces, without requiring access to its internals. For a Data Product, this distinction matters deeply. The platform does not own the data pipelines. It does not run the processing jobs. It governs the Data Product as a product: its contracts, its metadata, its lifecycle state. To do this well, the platform needs to see more than whether a specific task succeeded or failed. It needs to understand how the Data Product is behaving over time, whether that behavior matches its declared intent, and whether consumers can rely on it.

In the context of a Data Product Management Platform, observability serves a specific purpose. It aggregates signals from the data plane—execution runtimes, quality tools, processing engines—and surfaces them in the Control Plane as structured, governable information.

How the Platform Surfaces Observability Data

The Control Plane does not execute pipelines, and it does not directly observe runtime behavior at the execution level. That responsibility belongs to the data plane tools: orchestrators like Airflow or Dagster, quality frameworks like Soda or Great Expectations, and observability platforms purpose-built for data, such as Monte Carlo or Acceldata. The platform's role is different: it acts as the aggregation and governance layer for the signals these tools produce. Through the integration layer, observability signals flow into the Control Plane as structured events. A quality check failure becomes a governance-relevant event, not just a pipeline error. A freshness breach becomes a potential SLA violation. A lineage gap becomes a risk signal that may affect the trustworthiness of an entire downstream chain. The platform decides how these signals are classified, prioritized, and acted upon. This is what separates a data observability tool from platform-level observability. A tool can tell you that a column has nulls where there should be none. The platform can tell you that this breach affects three downstream Data Products, two of which are used for regulatory reporting, and that the owner of the upstream Data Product has been notified and the lifecycle state has been flagged accordingly.

SLO and SLA Integration

A Data Product communicates its promises through its contracts. Among these, the Service Level Objective and the Service Level Agreement are the most binding: they define the minimum level of behavior that consumers can depend on. An SLO is an internal commitment—the Data Product team pledges to maintain a specific level of quality, freshness, or availability. An SLA is the externalized form of that commitment: the promise made to consumers with governance weight behind it. Observability makes these promises measurable. Without observability signals flowing into the platform, SLAs are statements of intent. With them, they become verifiable claims. The platform tracks SLA compliance over time, reports breaches immediately, triggers notifications to affected consumers, and updates the trust state of the Data Product in the marketplace. This feedback loop is fundamental to building consumer confidence. Consumers who can see the real compliance history of a Data Product can make informed decisions. Governance teams that can observe SLA trends across the ecosystem can identify structural problems before they escalate into incidents.

Observability as Input to Governance and Lifecycle Decisions

The most important function of platform-level observability is what it feeds back into governance and lifecycle management. Observability signals are not passive records. They are active inputs into the decisions the platform makes. A Data Product that consistently misses its SLA may need to be flagged for review. A Data Product whose quality metrics have degraded beyond a defined threshold may trigger an automated governance workflow. This is what the logical architecture means when it describes observability as the place where runtime reality feeds back into governance. The Control Plane uses observability to close the loop between intent and execution. It transforms what would otherwise be a one-way flow—from design to deployment to consumption—into a continuous feedback cycle that keeps the platform aligned with what is actually happening in the data ecosystem. This feedback cycle also enables the platform to evolve its governance rules based on real evidence. Governance improves because it is grounded in reality rather than assumptions.

Cross-Cutting Concerns

Not every capability in a Data Product Management Platform belongs to a single module. Some concerns are so fundamental that they must cut across everything: lifecycle management, governance, operations, observability, and the marketplace. If implemented separately within each module, they would lead to inconsistent behavior. If they were ignored, the platform would lose the properties that make it safe to operate at scale. Three capabilities fall into this category: access control, communication, and audit. They are not features to be added as the platform matures. They are foundational properties of the Control Plane.

Access Control: Who Can Do What and Where

Role-Based Access Control (RBAC) is often understood as a technical security mechanism. In the context of a Data Product Management Platform, it is a more specific term: an instrument of governance. RBAC defines not only what users can do but also which roles have which responsibilities throughout the lifecycle of a Data Product. A Data Product team member has access to their product's descriptor and deployment controls. A governance officer has access to policy definitions and enforcement reports. A consumer has access to the marketplace and the Data Products to which they have been granted access. A platform operator has access to cross-cutting operational tooling.

Roles alone, however, are not sufficient. In a decentralized organization, a role without a scope is either too broad or too narrow. Saying that someone is an "administrator" or a "deployer" means nothing until you define what they administer or where they can deploy. This is where scoping becomes essential. A role must always be evaluated in the context of the scope to which it applies.

In practice, a Data Product Management Platform operates across several scope dimensions simultaneously.

The first and most intuitive is the organizational hierarchy. Permissions can apply globally, across all domains and all products. They can apply at the domain level—a team lead responsible for all data products within the Finance domain. They can apply at the level of a single data product or system—an engineer who owns the deployment of one specific product and nothing else. This hierarchical scoping mirrors the organizational structure and makes delegation natural: a domain owner can grant roles within their domain without requiring platform-wide authority.

The second scope dimension is geographic or regional. Large organizations, especially those operating across countries and business units, need to express permissions that cut across the hierarchy. For example, a governance officer who is responsible for all data products in the Finance domain, but only within the French subsidiary. Another example is a compliance specialist who must review every product operating under GDPR jurisdiction, regardless of domain. These regional scopes do not replace the organizational hierarchy; they intersect it. The access control model must support this intersection without requiring a separate permission structure for every combination.

The third scope dimension is the environment. A data product moves through multiple deployment stages—development, quality assurance, production—and the permissions appropriate for each stage differ significantly. An engineer may have full deployment authority in development and QA, where experimentation is expected and mistakes are recoverable. In production, the same engineer may be restricted to read-only access, with deployment authority reserved for a release manager or an automated pipeline that has passed governance checks. This is not a theoretical precaution. Uncontrolled production deployments are among the most common sources of incidents in data-intensive organizations. Environment-scoped RBAC makes the boundary between experimentation and production explicit and enforceable.

The fourth scope dimension is the technology landscape. Not all data products are built on the same stack. An organization may operate Databricks-based pipelines alongside AI systems, streaming platforms, and traditional warehousing solutions. An administrator of the Finance domain may have full authority over Databricks-based data products but no authority over AI workloads in the same domain. A machine learning engineer may have deployment rights for AI-specific products across multiple domains but no access to the underlying data pipelines that feed them. Technology-scoped access control reflects the reality that expertise and responsibility are often organized along technology lines rather than organizational ones.

These four dimensions—organizational hierarchy, geography, environment, and technology landscape—must compose. A single permission grant might specify: this user holds the deployer role, scoped to the Finance domain, restricted to the French region, limited to the production environment, and applicable only to Databricks-based data products. The access control engine evaluates all applicable scopes together. If any scope excludes the user, the action is denied.

This composability is what makes RBAC a governance instrument rather than just a security mechanism. It allows the platform to express access policies that mirror the organization's actual structure—its hierarchies, regional boundaries, technology choices, and risk appetite per environment—without collapsing everything into a flat list of permissions that no one can reason about. The design principle remains clear:

Roles are defined around responsibilities, not around individuals.

Scopes are defined around the boundaries that the organization considers meaningful. Access is granted to what each role needs to perform its function within those boundaries, and nothing more. RBAC must be granular enough to enforce meaningful distinctions, yet simple enough that teams understand what they can and cannot do. Overly complex permission models create confusion and invite shadow workarounds. The goal is precision without opacity.

Communication: Surfacing what Matters to Whom

The platform manages a constant flow of events: a Data Product has been deployed, a governance policy has been updated, a contract has been breached, and an SLA threshold has been crossed. Left unmanaged, this flow disappears into logs that nobody reads. Communication is the capability that ensures events reach the right stakeholders at the right time, in the right form.

This is not a notification system in the generic sense. It is a governed event distribution system aligned to the lifecycle and governance model of the platform. A lifecycle state change is relevant to the Data Product team and the responsible governance officer, but not necessarily to all consumers. A contract breach notification must be sent to affected consumers immediately, but the format and urgency depend on the nature of the breach. A governance policy update should reach platform architects and domain leads, but may also need to surface in the marketplace as a trust signal.

Communication must be configurable by role and event type, and it must be integrated with the same RBAC model that governs access. Sending a governance decision to someone without authority to act on it is noise. Failing to send it to someone who does is a risk. Done well, communication transforms the platform from a passive repository of governance state into an active system that keeps stakeholders informed and accountable, without burdening them with irrelevant information.

Audit: The History the Platform Cannot Lose

In regulated environments, accountability is not optional. In any environment where multiple teams manage Data Products that affect downstream consumers, accountability is foundational to trust. Audit is the capability that guarantees traceability: who performed which action, on which entity, at what time, and with what outcome.

This is not a logging exercise. Audit at the platform level is a governance capability. It records every significant lifecycle transition, every policy evaluation, every access grant or revocation, every governance decision taken or overridden. It does this in a tamper-resistant, queryable form that can support compliance reviews, incident investigations, and continuous improvement analyses.

The value of audit extends well beyond compliance. It enables organizational learning. When something goes wrong—a quality incident, a rogue deployment, an SLA breach that was not caught in time—audit provides the reconstruction trail. It answers not just what happened but what the decision process was that led there. It makes governance behavior visible, and therefore improvable.

In multi-team, multi-domain organizations, audit is also a social instrument. When every actor knows that their actions are recorded and attributable, the incentive to take shortcuts decreases and the habit of operating with care increases.

Governance Reporting Hooks

The three cross-cutting capabilities do not operate in isolation. They connect to a fourth concern: governance reporting. The platform accumulates a rich set of signals:

- Who accessed what?
- Which events were triggered?
- Which policies passed or failed?
- Which audit records were created?

This data must be accessible to governance teams in a structured, queryable form.

Governance reporting hooks are the mechanism through which this data is surfaced. They are not internal dashboards alone. They are outward-facing integration points that allow governance teams to extract compliance evidence, generate regulatory reports, and feed external audit systems.

In many organizations, data governance exists within a broader regulatory compliance framework that predates the Data Product Management Platform. The platform cannot function as an island. Its governance history must flow outward into the tools and processes that governance and compliance teams already use. This is what makes governance reporting hooks cross-cutting by nature: they must aggregate signals from lifecycle management, operations, observability, and marketplace interactions, and present them through a single, coherent reporting surface. Siloed reporting per module would require governance teams to join data from multiple sources to answer even basic questions about compliance status. A unified reporting surface eliminates that friction.

Why These Capabilities Must Be Cross-Cutting

The temptation, when building a platform incrementally, is to implement access control, communication, and audit inside each module as local features. This approach consistently leads to divergent behavior. The lifecycle module implements its own permission checks using a single model. The governance module develops another. The marketplace exposes data using yet another access control framework. Consumers and platform operators end up navigating inconsistent rules that change depending on which part of the platform they are working in. The same fragmentation repeats for audit: lifecycle events are logged one way, governance decisions another, marketplace interactions not at all. The audit trail becomes incomplete, and compliance reviews turn into painful reconciliation exercises.

By treating these three capabilities as cross-cutting concerns—implemented once and applied consistently across all modules—the platform achieves coherence.

A governance team can query the same audit trail regardless of whether the action happened in the factory, the lifecycle manager, or the marketplace. Access is evaluated by the same RBAC engine regardless of the entry point. Communication is routed by the same event system regardless of the source. This coherence is what makes the Control Plane governable at scale. Without it, the platform fragments into a collection of loosely related tools that happen to share a name.

The Role of the Platform in the AI Era

We are witnessing a fundamental shift in how software and data systems are built. Generative AI and coding agents in particular can produce code, infrastructure definitions, documentation, metadata, and data contracts at a speed that was unimaginable just a few years ago. This acceleration is real, and it dramatically changes the economics of implementation. Use cases that once required weeks of engineering effort can now be scaffolded in hours.

This is not a marginal improvement. It is a paradigm change. And, as with every paradigm shift, it creates a new set of problems for those who do not adapt their operating model to it.

The problem is straightforward. When implementation speed increases by an order of magnitude but governance remains manual and reactive, the gap between what is built and what is governed widens at an accelerating rate. Every data product created without embedded governance—without validated contracts, without architectural compliance, without proper metadata, without lifecycle controls—adds to a growing stock of governance debt. This debt is invisible at first. It becomes visible only when an audit fails, a consumer is impacted by a breaking change that was never detected, or a regulatory violation surfaces in production.

Manual governance models cannot absorb this acceleration. They were already struggling at human speed. At AI speed, they become structurally inadequate. If organizations embrace generative AI for data product development without simultaneously strengthening proactive, computational governance, they will accumulate governance debt faster than they have ever accumulated technical debt. And governance debt, unlike technical debt, carries regulatory and reputational consequences that cannot be ignored.

This is not a future risk. It is happening now. Organizations that allow AI-assisted development to proceed outside the boundaries of a governed platform are building faster, but they are building ungoverned.

The acceleration makes the consequences arrive sooner, not later.

The Control Plane as Guardian

The response to this challenge is not to slow down AI adoption. It is to ensure that the Control Plane becomes the authoritative guardian that shapes what AI produces.

A coding agent generating a data product must not operate in a vacuum. It must know which architectural blueprints apply. It must understand which governance policies are in force. It must respect the lifecycle stages and the validation gates that every data product must pass through. It must generate metadata that conforms to the organization's standards. It must produce infrastructure definitions that comply with security and compliance requirements. And it must do all of this not because a human reviews its output afterward, but because the platform provides the constraints and feedback loops that guide the agent towards correct behavior from the start.

This is the same principle that the rest of this book has argued for human teams: make the right thing the easiest thing to do. With AI agents, the principle becomes even more critical because the speed at which an unconstrained agent can diverge from organizational standards is orders of magnitude higher than a human team could ever achieve. A human engineer who ignores a governance guideline creates one non-compliant product. A coding agent that ignores the same guideline can create dozens before anyone notices.

In this model, the Control Plane serves a dual function. First, it provides the rules: computational policies, templates, blueprints, lifecycle definitions, and compliance requirements that constitute the organization's standards. Second, it provides a feedback loop: when the agent generates something that does not conform, the platform rejects it immediately with precise, actionable feedback, exactly as it would for a human-initiated deployment. The agent iterates, adjusts, and converges towards a compliant result.

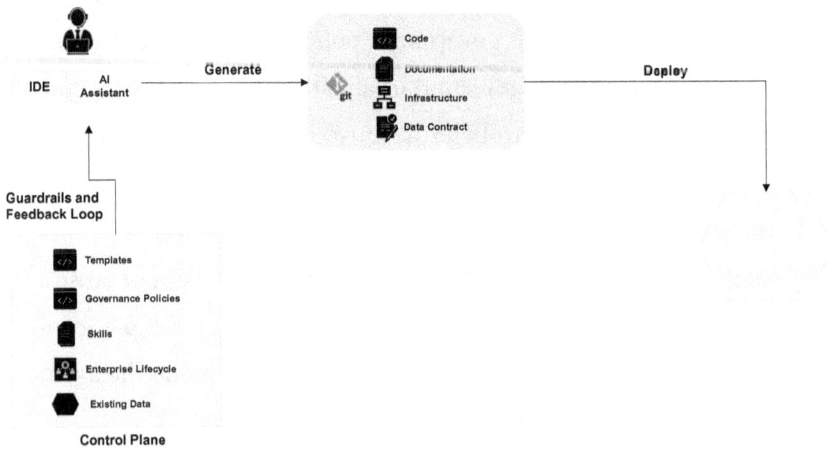

This is not a theoretical pattern. It mirrors exactly how CI/CD quality gates work for human developers. The difference is that the consumer of the feedback is now an agent rather than a person. The platform does not care who or what submits the deployment request. It evaluates the result against the same policies, contracts, and architectural rules. The governance is the same. Only the speed of iteration changes.

For this model to work, the Control Plane must be natively accessible to agents. This means every capability that matters for governance must be available as an API. Not as a user interface that an agent must scrape or simulate. Not as a document that an agent must parse and interpret. As a programmatic interface with clear contracts, versioned schemas, and deterministic behavior.

This is where the API-first design principle discussed acquires a new and urgent dimension. When the integration layer was designed, the primary consumers were CI/CD pipelines, orchestration engines, and human-operated tooling. Those consumers remain. But now a new class of consumer has emerged: the coding agent. And this consumer operates differently. It is faster, more literal, and has no tolerance for ambiguity. An API that returns a vague error message can be interpreted by a human who reads the documentation. An agent needs a structured, machine-readable response that it can act on programmatically.

The capabilities that must be exposed as APIs include, at a minimum: governance policy evaluation (Can this descriptor be deployed? Which rules does it violate?), template and blueprint retrieval (What is the recommended starting point for a data product of this type?), lifecycle state queries (What stage is this product in? What operations are permitted?), deployment and operations triggers (deploy, undeploy, version, rollback), metadata validation (Does this descriptor conform to the organization's metadata standards?), and contract validation (Does this output port respect the declared schema and SLA?).

MCP: Making the Control Plane Agent-Native

Beyond standard APIs, a more specific integration pattern deserves attention: the Model Context Protocol (MCP). MCP is an open standard that allows AI coding agents to discover and invoke external capabilities as part of their reasoning and generation process. Instead of the agent operating within its own knowledge and then submitting a result for validation, MCP allows the agent to call the platform's capabilities during generation—querying policies, retrieving templates, checking constraints, and validating intermediate results as it works.

This distinction matters. Without MCP or an equivalent mechanism, the interaction between the agent and the platform is sequential: generate, then validate, then fix, then validate again. With MCP, the interaction becomes conversational: the agent asks the platform what is expected, generates accordingly, checks its work against the platform's rules, and adjusts in real time. The convergence loop is tighter, faster, and produces fewer wasted iterations.

In concrete terms, exposing the Control Plane as an MCP server means that a coding agent generating a new data product can, during its generation process, retrieve the applicable governance policies for the target domain and environment, fetch the recommended template or blueprint for the product type, validate its generated descriptor against the platform's computational policies, check whether the proposed schema is compatible with existing consumers, and query the enterprise lifecycle to understand which metadata fields are mandatory at the current stage.

The agent does not need to have this knowledge built in. It does not need to be trained on the organization's specific rules. It discovers them at runtime through the protocol from the Control Plane, which is the authoritative source. This makes the pattern organization-agnostic. The same agent, connected to different Control Planes, produces data products that conform to different organizational standards.

The intelligence is in the platform, not in the agent.

The Fragmentation Risk

There is an alternative future that organizations must consciously avoid. Without a Control Plane that serves as the shared guardian, every data management tool in the ecosystem will develop its own AI agents. The data catalog vendor will ship an agent that knows how to generate catalog entries. The pipeline orchestrator will ship an agent that knows how to create pipelines. The data quality tool will ship an agent that knows how to define quality checks. The infrastructure platform will ship an agent that knows how to provision resources.

Each of these agents will be competent within its own perimeter. None of them will have a complete picture of the organization's interoperability rules, architectural standards, compliance requirements, quality expectations, and lifecycle conventions. None of them will know that a data product is not just a pipeline, or just a catalog entry, or just a set of quality checks. It is a governed system that spans all of these concerns.

This is the tool fragmentation problem we already talked about, reproduced at AI speed. The same mistake—believing that tools alone can solve structural problems—now plays out with agents instead of platforms. Technology changes. The failure mode does not.

The result is predictable. AI-generated artifacts that are locally correct but globally inconsistent. Pipelines that work but violate architectural standards. Quality checks that pass within the quality tool but do not align with the data contracts declared in the Control Plane. Infrastructure that is provisioned but does not conform to the security policies that apply to the target environment and domain.

The Control Plane prevents this fragmentation by serving as the single source of truth for organizational standards. When every agent—regardless of which vendor built it—queries the same Control Plane for policies, templates, and lifecycle rules, the outputs converge. Not because the agents are coordinated with each other, but because they are all constrained by the same boundaries. The Control Plane does not need to know which agent is calling it. It enforces the same rules regardless of the caller. Convergence emerges from shared constraints, not from centralized orchestration.

The platform does not replace these specialized agents. It governs them. It provides the guardrails and feedback loops that ensure every agent, regardless of its origin, produces artifacts that are compliant, interoperable, and governed by design. The Control Plane becomes the gravitational field that keeps a constellation of autonomous agents in orbit rather than letting them drift into incoherent directions.

Key Takeaways

The platform must treat agents as first-class consumers. This means structured, machine-readable error responses. It means deterministic behavior that agents can rely on for their convergence loops. It means rate limiting and access control that accommodate the interaction patterns of agents, which are more frequent but simpler on an individual basis than human interactions.

The stakes are higher than they appear. AI does not just accelerate delivery. It accelerates consequences. Every decision that was tolerable at human speed—a missing metadata field, a non-standard architecture, an undeclared breaking change—becomes a systemic risk when multiplied by the throughput of AI-assisted development. The platform's role is to ensure that this acceleration produces governed value rather than ungoverned chaos.

FIVE

People, Journeys, and Reality

A platform is a product. Like any product, it must choose which problems to solve and how to deliver value to them. A platform built for "everyone" in the abstract serves no one in practice. It succeeds when it understands exactly who it serves and how it transforms their daily work.

One of the most recurring questions I get from large organizations is deceptively simple: who are the platform's personas, and what skills do they need? The question matters because understanding how a platform fits into the skills and journeys of real people is the difference between adoption and being routed around.

In data product management, five personas stand out as the core audience: the Data Product Team, the Platform Team, the Domain Owner, the Governance Team, and the Data Consumer. Each has a different vantage point. Each speaks a slightly different language. Each measures value in their own way.

These are not static roles. They are dynamic actors whose paths often intersect, whose needs sometimes align and sometimes conflict. A well-designed platform does not erase these tensions. It manages them, creating the conditions for autonomy and governance to coexist.

In every company, each of these five personas had a different story about the platform. The distance between those stories—and the work needed to align them—defined what adoption actually meant in practice.

The chapters that follow examine each persona in turn: what their work looks like before the platform, what changes when the platform is in place, and what determines whether they adopt it or route around it.

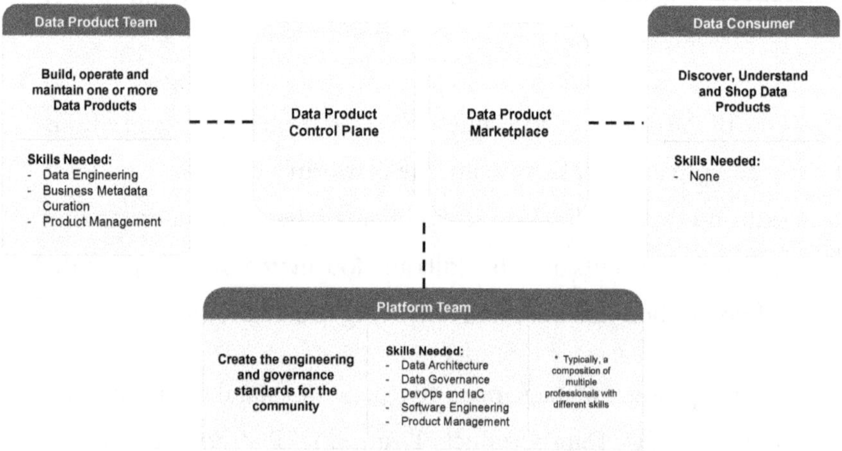

Data Product Team

Who They Are

A Data Product Team is inherently cross-functional. It brings together backend and data engineers, data scientists or analysts, data modelers, quality specialists, DevOps or platform-savvy engineers, and a Data Product Owner who orchestrates the work and represents the business perspective. The team may sit within a business domain, but its output—the data product—often serves multiple consumers across the enterprise.

Some teams operate in a project-based model, forming temporarily to deliver a specific output and then disbanding. Others embrace product thinking, staying intact over the long term to iterate and adapt the same data product to evolving needs. The platform must support both, without forcing an organizational choice.

What They Care About

The team's priorities are practical: deliver a product that solves a real problem for consumers, build it in a way that is maintainable, observable, and trustworthy, move quickly from concept to production without getting trapped in bureaucracy, and retain enough flexibility to use the right tools for the job while respecting governance constraints. In short: velocity without chaos. Freedom without risk.

Life Before the Platform

Before the enabling platform, the Data Product Team's work often began with a blank page and a maze of dependencies. Setting up infrastructure was a scavenger hunt: Who can create a database schema? Where do we host the processing jobs? Which Jenkins instance is the "right" one? Someone remembered a Terraform module in an internal Git repository, but it was undocumented and half-broken. Policies existed, but they were scattered across Confluence pages, often outdated, and no one could confirm if they were still current.

On top of this, business requirements and technical analysis traveled back and forth in an endless exchange of Excel files sent via email. These spreadsheets contained everything—business rules, field mappings, database schemas, even pseudo-code for transformation logic. They were meant to foster shared understanding among business analysts, engineers, and stakeholders, but in practice, they became a minefield. Mistakes inevitably crept in: a column renamed in one version but not in another, a data type mismatch, a transformation formula that only made sense to the person who wrote it. There was no version control. The team relied on filenames like Mapping_FINAL_v3_revised_LAST.xlsx to track progress, but with multiple parallel email threads, it was impossible to know which version was the source of truth. By the time the product reached production—after countless revisions of both Excel and code—no one could say with certainty which set of requirements the live system was actually implementing. A defect reported by a consumer could trigger a forensic investigation, trying to reconcile what was running in production with the half-dozen "final" requirement spreadsheets still circulating.

The challenges did not end at go-live. Curation was ad hoc and inconsistent. Product descriptions for the internal catalog were often written after deployment, sometimes by people who had not worked directly on the product. Data masking rules, quality thresholds, and SLAs were recorded in separate documents, if at all. The result was that consumers discovered products without clear usage guidelines or reliable guarantees, leading to misunderstandings and support requests that consumed more of the team's time.

Validation, when it happened, was late in the process and often manual. Governance teams ran checks after deployment, sometimes forcing rollbacks or urgent hotfixes when non-compliance was detected. This created friction between delivery and governance, with both sides frustrated by the timing and the lack of shared visibility.

Once in production, operations were reactive. Problems were usually discovered when a consumer complained, not because there was a reliable way to monitor freshness, quality, or contract compliance. Fixes required filing tickets with other teams, waiting for approvals, and coordinating changes across multiple systems—slowing down responses and eroding trust.

When changes were needed, managing evolution was risky and opaque. The team often did not know exactly who was using the product, how it was being consumed, or what might break if they altered a schema or changed a transformation. Communication about changes was informal, and deprecations were rarely announced in advance, leaving consumers to discover breaking changes the hard way.

In short, the pre-platform journey was one of constant friction: slow starts, unclear requirements, late-stage surprises, reactive firefighting, and change management without visibility. The business wanted insights and agility; the team spent most of its energy managing the noise around delivery rather than delivering sustained value.

From Idea to Build

With the platform in place, the starting point changes fundamentally. A data product does not begin with a command to "start coding." It begins inside the platform's lifecycle management, with a structured conversation about why the product should exist, who will use it, and how it connects to the organization's strategic priorities. The platform provides a space where the business case is formalized, linked to measurable outcomes, and tied to real stakeholders who will rely on the result. From the very first step, the team knows where they are in the lifecycle, what the next step is, and who needs to act.

Requirements are captured in a single, version-controlled, machine-readable format that analysts, engineers, and governance can all work with. The fragile Excel files circulating by email—full of mismatched mappings and hidden errors—are replaced by a source of truth that can be validated from day one. There is never a question about which version is current. The team is already operating inside the platform.

Once the "why" and "what" are agreed upon, the team selects a blueprint and a template from the platform's factory. The blueprint encodes the architecture—storage patterns, output port types, orchestration strategy—while the template provides a concrete starting point: a repository with a standard structure, a preconfigured CI/CD pipeline, logging already wired in, a stub data contract, and observability endpoints ready to emit signals. Instead of debating folder structures, connection management, or which Jenkins instance to use, the team inherits decisions that have already been made and validated. The blank page disappears. What remains is business logic.

From this point, the team iterates—and the platform is present at every iteration. An engineer writes a dbt model that transforms customer data. Within minutes, the CI/CD pipeline runs, and a computational policy detects that the output schema does not match the data contract declared in the descriptor. The pipeline does not silently pass. It stops and explains: "Field customer_region is declared as non-nullable in the contract but the transformation produces nulls for 12% of rows." The engineer fixes the transformation, pushes again, and the policy passes. This feedback loop runs on every commit. It is not a gate at the end. It is a companion throughout.

Another engineer adds a new source table to the pipeline. A policy checks whether the source is a registered data product and whether the team has an active access agreement for it. The check fails: the source exists, but there is no agreement in place. The platform tells the engineer exactly what is missing and links to the marketplace where the access request can be made.

Dependencies are not discovered in production when something breaks.
They are surfaced during development, when fixing them is cheap.

A data scientist contributes a scoring model as part of the product. A security policy scans the dependencies and flags a library with a known vulnerability. The feedback is immediate: "Library X version 2.3.1 has CVE-2025-XXXX. Approved alternative: version 2.4.0." The scientist updates the dependency and moves on. The vulnerability never reaches production.

Development is iterative and collaborative. Engineers write transformation code, analysts validate outputs against requirements, data scientists contribute domain-specific metrics, and the Data Product Owner ensures alignment with the original purpose. Every change passes through automated tests—unit tests for transformation logic, data quality checks, contract validation against declared schemas, and governance policies—all running side by side in the same CI/CD pipeline. Version control tracks the evolution of the product, with branching strategies that let multiple people work in parallel. Governance runs continuously, from the first commit to the last.

Curation

Curation is where the raw technical build becomes something discoverable, understandable, and trustworthy. It is not an afterthought. It is the process of making the product ready for the people who will consume it—and the platform makes sure it actually happens.

The entire cross-functional team participates in curation. It is not the domain of a single role. A functional analyst opens the platform's curation interface—not an IDE, not a YAML editor, not a Git branch—and starts enriching the product's metadata. The interface must be designed for inclusivity: easier and more functional than the Excel sheets of the past. Excel was flexible but chaotic. The platform keeps the good—ease of editing, accessibility for non-technical users—while adding what Excel could never provide: structured validation, built-in governance checks, automatic traceability, and a single source of truth always in sync with the deployed product.

As the analyst works, the platform provides continuous feedback. She links output port fields to business concepts in the enterprise ontology, so the product will appear in marketplace searches by business term rather than just by technical name. Midway through, a policy flags that three fields in the main output port lack descriptions and links to the glossary. The message is specific: "Fields invoice_date, net_amount, and tax_code in port customer_invoices are not linked to any business concept. Consumers will not be able to discover this product by business term." She adds the descriptions and the links. The policy passes.

Next, the platform checks lineage completeness. A policy reports that two of the four declared input sources are not connected in the lineage graph. The analyst sees exactly which sources are missing and adds the lineage connections. Impact analysis—who depends on what—becomes possible only because lineage is complete. The platform prevents incomplete lineage from reaching consumers.

On the compliance side, policies verify that data masking rules are in place for every field flagged as sensitive. A data deletion policy checks whether the product implements the required deletion pattern for personally identifiable data. If the pattern is missing, the platform blocks progression to the next lifecycle state and explains why: "This data product contains PII fields but does not implement a deletion procedure. GDPR compliance requires a documented deletion mechanism before production release."

Operational commitments are validated at this stage. The analyst declares SLAs—freshness, availability, response times. A policy immediately flags that the freshness SLA is missing for the primary output port. Another checks that the declared SLA is realistic, given the refresh frequency configured in the orchestration. Usage agreements are attached, clarifying what consumers are permitted to do with the data, under which conditions, and with what restrictions. These agreements are version-controlled like the rest of the descriptor.

Usage examples, sample queries, and connection instructions are provided for each output port. By the end of curation, the product tells the truth. Anyone who discovers it in the marketplace can understand what it does, trust its commitments, and start using it without guesswork.

Validation

When the team believes the product is ready for its first release, they request a lifecycle transition. The platform runs the full set of computational policies defined for that transition—not through a review meeting, but through automated, deterministic checks. The result is precise: every policy that passed, every policy that failed, and for each failure, the reason and the path to resolution.

A product that reaches this point with incomplete metadata, missing SLAs, unresolved security findings, or contract violations cannot advance. But the team was never surprised. Every one of these checks ran during development and curation. The validation gate is a confirmation, not a discovery. This is where trust in the platform—and in the governance process behind it—is either reinforced or eroded. An opaque rejection that arrives too late to address without major disruption is the fastest way to lose a team's confidence. The platform prevents this by making the rules visible from the first day.

Release

Releasing a data product is a moment of exposure. The team makes a public commitment to the rest of the organization: this product is ready to be used. The platform ensures that consumers only see the product when it is complete, coherent, and consistent with the promises made during design and curation. Partial or accidental releases are prevented by design.

A release is not only about delivering code and data. It is about publishing the product's description, contracts, and guarantees in the marketplace. Once live, consumers encounter the product exactly as intended: understandable, discoverable, and trustworthy from the first interaction. The marketplace page reads like a real product page—purpose, owner, SLA commitments, quality guarantees, sample queries, lineage, and consumer ratings—because the curation process made all of this real, not decorative.

Operations

Once the product is in production, the priority shifts from building to keeping promises. The platform's observability layer aggregates signals from the data plane—pipeline execution logs, quality check results, freshness metrics, volume trends—and surfaces them as structured, governable information in the Control Plane.

This is not passive monitoring. The platform evaluates these signals against the product's declared SLAs and contracts. When freshness drifts beyond the committed threshold, the platform does not wait for a consumer to complain. It flags the breach, notifies the team, and updates the product's trust state in the marketplace. Consumers who check the product's page see the real compliance history—not a static promise, but a living record of whether promises are being kept.

When issues arise, the team can respond directly through the platform: pausing an output port, replaying a data window, triggering a reprocessing job, or rolling forward to a corrected version. These are self-service operations—no ticket queues, no approval chains, no coordination across multiple systems. Traces and lineage allow the team to track data through every transformation to identify where something went wrong. A quality degradation in a downstream product can be traced back through the lineage graph to the specific upstream change that caused it. Observability also feeds back into governance. A product that consistently misses its SLA may be flagged for review. A product whose quality metrics have degraded beyond a defined threshold may trigger an automated governance workflow. The platform closes the loop between what was promised at design time and what is actually happening in production.

Change Management

Change is inevitable. Markets shift, data sources are replaced, new regulatory requirements appear, and consumers request enhancements that were never foreseen at launch. A data product must adapt and improve, but every change carries risk.

The platform makes this tractable. The team has a clear map of consumers, the contracts in place, and the dependencies that connect products across domains. Before releasing a new version, the impact is visible: who will be affected, how many consumers, and which downstream products depend on it. A policy detects that a column rename in the new version will break three existing consumer contracts. The platform reports the specific contracts, fields, and consumers affected. The team can decide to negotiate a migration path or to publish the new version alongside the old one, giving consumers time to adapt.

Versioning mechanics handle the rest. Minor versions support backward-compatible improvements. Major versions introduce intentional breaking changes and require explicit change management, consumer awareness, and often coexistence with previous versions during a transition period. Deprecation announcements are published in the marketplace with a timeline. Consumers discover upcoming changes before they happen, not after something breaks.

Change management becomes a natural extension of product ownership—the act of steering the product's future while keeping the ecosystem stable.

The platform does not remove the difficulty of change.
It removes the blindness.

What Success Looks Like

The team ships faster with fewer surprises. They spend their time on business logic rather than plumbing. Every friction point that used to consume weeks—environment setup, governance reviews, compliance checks, consumer communication—is handled by the platform as a continuous, embedded part of the workflow. Governance is not something that happens to them. It is something that runs alongside them, catching problems while they are still cheap to fix. They carry real ownership because the platform gives them the tools, the visibility, and the feedback to act on it.

Platform Team

Who They Are

The Platform Team designs, builds, and maintains the enabling platform that allows data products to be conceived, delivered, and evolved at scale. They do not produce data products themselves.

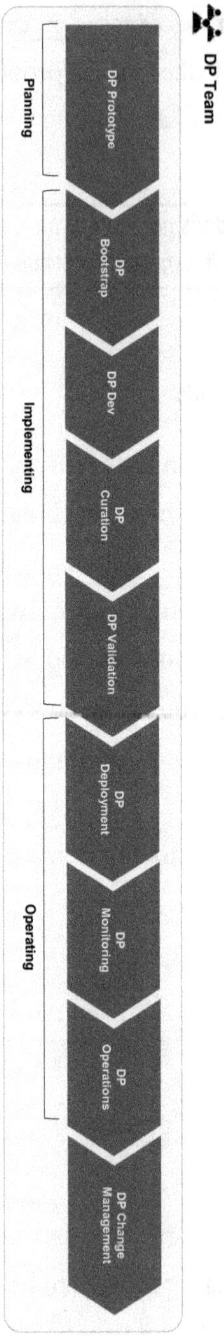

Data Product Life-cycle

Their mission is to make it possible for Data Product Teams, governance functions, and data consumers to collaborate within a single, coherent environment. They operate at the intersection of technology, process, and people. This position requires them to think not only about what works technically, but also about what is intuitive for every role in the ecosystem.

What They Care About

The Platform Team's priorities are rooted in a balancing act: giving delivery teams the freedom to move quickly without compromising security, reliability, or compliance. In practice, this means consistency (a standardized, predictable environment that works the same way for every team), automation (removing manual bottlenecks so engineers spend time on business value, not repetitive tasks), scalability (supporting new workloads, domains, and technologies without major rewrites), governance by design (embedding policies and controls into workflows so compliance is a natural outcome), and visibility (a unified view of platform health, usage, and performance to anticipate problems before they escalate).

Life Before the Platform

Before the platform matured into a coherent environment, the Platform Team's days were dominated by firefighting and manual work. Requests for new environments, pipelines, or databases came in through scattered tickets, chat messages, or hallway conversations—each one unique, each requiring a different sequence of approvals and manual interventions.

Provisioning was slow and inconsistent. Scripts to spin up infrastructure lived in personal folders or outdated wikis, often written for a one-off use case and never updated. There was no single way to create a development environment or deploy a data pipeline. Each team had its own approach, and the Platform Team had to support them all.

Governance rules existed, but they were detached from delivery. They were stored in PDFs on shared drives or in Confluence pages that no one was sure were still up to date. Enforcement happened late, often after a product had gone live, forcing painful rollbacks or urgent fixes.

The monitoring landscape was a patchwork of tools and dashboards, each covering a piece of the picture but never the whole. The Platform Team could detect when something was broken—usually because a consumer complained—but rarely saw the early warning signs. Changes to shared components were risky. Without a full map of dependencies, a seemingly small update could break multiple products. Notifications to affected teams were ad hoc, and recovery plans were often improvised under pressure. In short, life before the platform was a world of slow starts, unpredictable delivery, reactive governance, and operational fragility. The Platform Team knew they could do better—but only if they shifted from being a reactive service desk to a proactive product team.

Data Product Team Experience

The Platform Team's first responsibility is designing the experience for Data Product Teams. This starts with blueprints and templates. A blueprint encodes the architecture of a data product—storage patterns, output port types, orchestration strategy—while a template provides a concrete starting point: a repository skeleton, a preconfigured CI/CD pipeline, logging already wired in, a stub data contract, and observability endpoints ready to emit signals. The Platform Team curates a small, well-reasoned set of these—not one for every conceivable use case, but the 20% that covers 80% of needs.

The measure of success is practical. A Data Product Team selects the "Customer Data Pipeline (dbt)" template. Within minutes, they have a working repository with a standard structure, embedded data quality checks, and governance policies already hooked into the pipeline. They never ask "Which Jenkins instance?" or "Where is the Terraform module?" because the template made those decisions for them. If the Platform Team has done its job, onboarding a new data product takes minutes, not days, and the team can focus almost entirely on business logic from the first commit.

Data Product Lifecycle

One of the Platform Team's most consequential responsibilities is implementing the lifecycle workflow for every data product, from idea to retirement. In most large organizations, a data product does not jump from concept to production in a straight line. It navigates a sequence of approvals, validations, and integrations that involve multiple stakeholders: budget approvals through the ERP, architectural reviews with the Enterprise Architecture team, security assessments, governance board sign-offs, environment provisioning, and dataset registration. Each step belongs to a different team and follows a different process.

Before the platform, this sequence existed as documentation—flowcharts in PowerPoint, checklists in Confluence, tribal knowledge in people's heads. Teams stumbled through it, asking, "What do I do next?" at every turn. The Platform Team's job is to turn this sequence into an executable, navigable workflow inside the platform.

In practice, this means defining the lifecycle as a state machine: a data product starts in a "planning" state, moves through "draft," "implementing," "quality assurance," and "production," and eventually reaches "retired." Each transition has preconditions—computational policies that must be satisfied, approvals that must be granted, integrations that must be completed. The Platform Team configures these transitions to reflect the organization's actual processes, not an idealized version. If budget approval requires a call to the ERP system, the platform integrates with the ERP. If architectural review requires sign-off from a specific role, the platform routes the request and tracks the response. The result is that a data product team always knows where they are in the lifecycle, what the next step is, what conditions must be satisfied, and who is responsible for moving things forward. The platform does not replace the enterprise processes. It connects and orchestrates them into a coherent journey. This is what separates real self-service from "here are some tools, figure the rest out yourself."

The lifecycle workflow is not static. As governance models change, technologies evolve, or organizational structures shift, the Platform Team updates the workflow configuration. A new compliance requirement—say, a mandatory AI ethics review for products that feed machine learning models—can be added as a new transition condition without rewriting the platform. The lifecycle is configurable and evolvable by design, because the Platform Team knows that what works today will not be sufficient next year.

Infrastructure Automation

Provisioning infrastructure is no longer a bottleneck. A data product team triggers a deployment through the platform. Under the hood, the platform interprets the data product descriptor, infers the required components and their dependencies, and orchestrates provisioning in the correct order—storage first, then compute, then output ports. No ticket queues, no manual handovers, no undocumented Terraform scripts circulating across Git repositories.

The Platform Team designs this experience so that deployment feels like a one-click operation, even when it triggers dozens of coordinated actions. But abstraction does not mean opacity. When a deployment step fails, the platform does not expose a raw Terraform error, forcing the team to learn infrastructure tooling. It translates the error into something contextualized and actionable: "Storage provisioning failed because the requested region is not enabled for this subscription. Contact your cloud administrator or select an alternative region." If the error is unresolvable by the data product team, the platform routes it to the Platform Team with full context already attached—no back-and-forth to reproduce the issue.

Rollback is a first-class capability. When a new version of a data product causes problems, the platform can quickly and safely restore the previous version. The Platform Team does not get a panicked Slack message asking for help. The data product team rolls back autonomously, and the platform records what happened, when, and why.

DevOps Integration

The CI/CD pipeline is not bolted on after the fact. It is baked into every template the Platform Team provides. Every commit to a data product repository triggers a pipeline that runs functional tests, data quality checks, contract validation, security scans, and governance policies—all in the same execution. These pipelines are the backbone of consistent delivery. The Platform Team hooks computational policies into these pipelines so that governance feedback reaches the developer within minutes of a commit. A schema mismatch with the data contract, a missing SLA declaration, an unapproved library—all of these surface immediately, with specific messages and resolution paths. The developer never needs to ask "Why did my build fail?"—the pipeline tells them.

The pipelines are configurable. Teams can extend them without breaking core standards. But the Platform Team designs the defaults so that following the standard path takes less effort than bypassing it. Compliance becomes the natural choice, not because it is enforced by policing, but because it is easier than the alternative.

Lifecycle Operations

Beyond build and release, the Platform Team ensures that every operational action a data product team needs is available as a self-service capability within the platform. Deploying, upgrading, rolling back, pausing an output port, replaying a data window, triggering reprocessing, retiring a product—all of these are explicit, auditable operations mediated by the Control Plane.

The observability layer aggregates signals from the data plane—pipeline execution logs, quality check results, freshness metrics, volume trends—and surfaces them as structured, governable information. The Platform Team configures how these signals are classified and prioritized. A freshness breach becomes a potential SLA violation. A quality check failure becomes a governance-relevant event that can trigger automated workflows. The platform evaluates signals against declared contracts and updates the trust state of data products in the marketplace—without the Platform Team being in the loop for every incident.

The real measure is proactive stability. The Platform Team monitors platform-level health—adoption rates, lead times from idea to production, deployment success rates, bottleneck identification—not individual data product incidents. When a pattern emerges—say, a cluster of deployment failures all traced to the same infrastructure provider API change—the Platform Team fixes it at the platform level, and every data product team benefits.

Governance Policies Integration

The Platform Team does not write governance rules in isolation. They implement the policies designed by the Governance Team as computational checks—machine-readable, deterministic, and embedded in the delivery workflow. A policy that says "every data product must declare an SLA for its primary output port" becomes an automated check that runs during curation and again at the lifecycle transition to production. A policy that says "PII fields must have a deletion procedure" becomes a validation that blocks deployment if the procedure is missing.

These policies cover far more than data protection. They include architectural constraints (approved blueprint patterns, data modeling standards), security requirements (dependency vulnerability scanning, approved library registries), metadata completeness (every output port field linked to the business glossary), and operational commitments (SLAs validated against actual refresh frequencies). The Platform Team maintains the policy execution engine. The Governance Team defines what the policies check. Data product teams experience them as immediate, specific feedback—not as a separate governance review happening weeks later.

Data Consumers Experience

The Platform Team also designs the marketplace—the interface through which consumers discover, evaluate, and request access to data products. Discovery is powered by business metadata, not technical field names. Consumers search with terms from the enterprise ontology and find products, not raw tables. Each product page shows purpose, owner, SLA history, quality metrics, sample queries, lineage, and consumer ratings.

When a consumer requests access, the platform routes the approval to the appropriate owner or automatically applies the relevant policy. ACL changes are applied without manual IT intervention. The consumer sees progress in real time—no silent email threads, no weeks-long waits. If the product supports multiple output protocols, the consumer chooses the one that fits their stack from within the marketplace.

Some consumers eventually become prosumers—people who consume data as an ingredient for building something new. The Platform Team designs the transition from consumption to production to be seamless: a consumer who decides to build a data product on top of what they discovered finds their access agreements already in place and the lineage connections already visible.

Release and Change Management

Releasing platform capabilities is as critical as releasing data products. When the Platform Team introduces a new template, updates a governance policy, or changes an infrastructure component, the same principles apply: impacts are understood before changes happen, affected teams are notified in advance, and migrations are supported with clear guidance.

The platform publishes change announcements through the same notification mechanism used for data product changes. When a new policy version will be enforced, the Platform Team runs simulations to show which existing data products would be affected and communicates the timeline: awareness first, warnings during a grace period, and enforcement after teams have had time to adapt.

Platform evolution is a partnership, not a disruption.

What Success Looks Like

Data product teams launch faster without last-minute surprises. Environments work the same way for every team. Governance feedback reaches developers during development, not after deployment. Operations are proactive—issues are spotted before consumers notice them. The Platform Team spends its time improving the platform as a product, not firefighting individual data product incidents. Adoption grows because the platform makes teams' lives easier, not because it was mandated.

Domain Owner

Who They Are

The Domain Owner is accountable for the overall value and health of their domain's portfolio of data products. They do not write code, but they decide what to build, what to retire, and how each product aligns with business objectives. They are responsible for ensuring that the domain's investments deliver measurable outcomes and that its commitments to other domains are upheld. In contexts where an organization does not adopt a domain-oriented structure, this role is often performed by a Portfolio Manager. The same principles apply whether the focus is on long-lived products or on shorter-term projects: overseeing the portfolio, aligning delivery with strategic goals, and ensuring that resources are invested where they can deliver the greatest value.

What They Care About

They care about visibility across their portfolio—knowing which products are live, which are in development, how they are performing against SLAs, and how they are being used. They need to avoid duplication of effort, direct investment toward the highest-value opportunities, and maintain trust between their domain and its consumers. They need a clear understanding of dependencies, so that changes are made with foresight rather than guesswork.

Life Before the Platform

Before the enabling platform, visibility was fragmented. Information about products lived in spreadsheets, slide decks, and scattered wiki pages, often out of date or incomplete. Duplication was common—different teams building similar products without knowing the other existed. Consumer feedback was sporadic and informal, making it hard to measure impact or justify further investment.

When cross-domain commitments were made, there was no clear way to track whether the agreed-upon data was being delivered reliably. Decisions about what to fund or retire were often political rather than evidence-based, and change management was risky because the impact on consumers was rarely known in advance.

With the Platform in Place

The platform gives the Domain Owner something they never had before: a single, live view of their entire portfolio.

They open the platform's domain dashboard and see every data product in their domain—live, in development, and retired—with current lifecycle state, SLA compliance history, consumer count, and usage trends. No more assembling this picture from spreadsheets and slide decks. The information is not a snapshot someone prepared for a quarterly review. It is the actual state, updated continuously from the Control Plane.

Duplication becomes visible. The dashboard shows that two teams in the same domain are building products with overlapping schemas and overlapping consumers. Before the platform, neither team knew the other existed. Now the Domain Owner can intervene early: merge the efforts, or differentiate the products explicitly so consumers know which one to use. The platform does not make this decision—it makes the decision possible by surfacing the overlap.

Every product in the portfolio is linked to its stated business objectives. The Domain Owner can see not just that a product is live, but whether it is actually being consumed, by how many teams, and for what purposes. A product with zero consumers after three months raises a different question than one with 30. Investment decisions—what to fund, what to retire, what to enhance—are grounded in evidence, not in the loudest voice in the room.

When a cross-domain commitment exists (e.g., the Sales domain promises to deliver customer data to the Risk domain with specific freshness and quality guarantees), the platform formalizes that commitment as a contract. The Domain Owner does not need to chase email threads to know whether the promise is being kept. The contract's compliance history is visible: SLA met for the last ninety days, one breach two weeks ago, root cause identified and resolved. When the Risk domain asks "Can we depend on this?", the answer is backed by data, not by reassurance.

Before approving a change to a high-impact product, the Domain Owner checks the platform's impact analysis. The platform shows exactly who will be affected: 14 consumers across three domains, two of which feed regulatory reports. The Domain Owner sees the specific contracts that would break and the specific fields involved. This is not a guess. It is a deterministic computation from the dependency graph that the platform maintains. The decision to proceed, postpone, or negotiate a migration path is informed, not blind.

What Success Looks Like

Fewer but higher-quality products, each with clear business impact. Investments flow toward initiatives with measurable outcomes. Duplication drops because overlaps are visible and addressed early. Consumers trust the domain because commitments are kept, and when change happens, it is planned, communicated, and managed deliberately.

Data Governance Team

Who They Are

The Data Governance Team is responsible for ensuring that the organization's data ecosystem is safe, compliant, and aligned with agreed standards—without slowing down delivery. They do not build data products, but they shape the environment in which those products are designed, developed, and operated. They define the rules of the game, ensuring those rules are clear, enforceable, and consistently applied.

In a modern platform context, governance shifts from being an after-the-fact inspection to becoming an integral, computational part of the delivery process. Governance practitioners work alongside delivery and platform teams to design policies that safeguard security, privacy, quality, and interoperability while respecting the realities of product development.

They are also responsible for ensuring semantic interoperability across the ecosystem. This means verifying that all data products use the business glossary or enterprise ontology correctly, so that shared concepts are represented consistently. By enforcing these semantic standards, they ensure that data products can be combined, compared, and integrated without misunderstandings—enabling true cross-domain data reuse and trust.

What They Care About

The Data Governance Team is committed to ensuring security, privacy, and compliance without hindering innovation. They need policies expressed as code—unambiguous, enforceable, and aligned with business risk appetite. They need trust across the ecosystem, which requires rules that are visible, consistent, and fairly applied. They need governance tailored to context, recognizing that what matters for a reporting package may differ from what matters for a machine learning agent or a real-time data product. And they need compliance that is measurable and transparent, so that audits are based on facts rather than manual reporting.

Life Before the Platform

Before the enabling platform, governance was a separate function, sitting apart from delivery. They inspected work only after it was complete, issuing reports and recommendations that sometimes arrived too late to act on without major disruption. Guidelines existed, but they were buried in static documents, inconsistently interpreted, and frequently ignored. Enforcement was manual, relying on self-reported spreadsheets or ad hoc reviews.

This created friction with delivery teams, who saw governance as "the team that says no" rather than a partner in building safe, reliable products. New policies were sometimes introduced abruptly, without time for teams to adapt, causing delays, rework, and frustration. Auditors struggled to get a clear picture of the ecosystem, and governance lacked real-time insight into compliance or risk.

With the Platform in Place

The Governance Team's work changes at the root. Instead of writing policies in documents and hoping teams read them, governance practitioners author computational policies—machine-readable rules that the platform executes automatically. A policy is no longer a paragraph in a PDF. It is code that runs inside the CI/CD pipeline, during curation, at lifecycle transitions, and at runtime. Consider a concrete example. The Governance Team defines a policy: "Every data product that contains personally identifiable information must implement a data deletion procedure before reaching production." In the old world, this rule lived in a Confluence page. Some teams read it, some did not. Compliance was discovered—or not—during an audit months later. Now, the platform evaluates this policy every time a data product requests a lifecycle transition to production. If the deletion procedure is missing, the transition is blocked, and the team receives a specific explanation: "This data product contains PII fields but does not implement a deletion procedure. GDPR compliance requires a documented deletion mechanism before production release." The Governance Team never needs to chase the issue. The platform enforces it.

Every policy is accompanied by a readable rationale that explains why it exists and the trade-offs it implies. This is deliberate. A policy that blocks a deployment without explanation breeds resentment. A policy that explains itself builds understanding.

The Governance Team invests in writing these rationales because they know that a rule understood is a rule respected.

Policies are tuned to specific system types. The governance needs of a batch data product that feeds regulatory reports differ from those of a real-time streaming product that powers a dashboard. The platform's metamodel allows the Governance Team to target policies precisely. This policy applies to all data products of type "regulatory reporting" and to products classified as "internal analytics." Not everything is governed the same way, and the platform makes this selectivity explicit rather than buried in exception lists.

New policies do not appear without warning. When the Governance Team designs a new rule—say, "every output port must have at least one usage example and one sample query"—they do not flip a switch and block every non-compliant product overnight. Instead, they use the platform to run simulations. The platform evaluates the new policy against every existing data product and reports the results: seventy-two products would pass, eighteen would fail, and the failures cluster in three domains that historically have sparse documentation.

Armed with this information, the Governance Team communicates the upcoming change to the affected domains, sets a 60-day grace period during which the platform flags violations as warnings without blocking delivery, and provides guidance on how to comply. When enforcement begins, the community already knows what to expect. Nobody is surprised.

Obsolete policies are retired with the same care. A policy that no longer applies, perhaps because a regulation changed or a technology was decommissioned, is explicitly phased out. The platform shows which products it governs and confirms that the removal does not create gaps.

The platform executes governance checks at multiple points in the lifecycle: during development (in the CI/CD pipeline), during curation (as the team enriches metadata and declares contracts), at lifecycle transitions (when a product moves from draft to QA to production), and at runtime (when observability signals indicate a drift from declared behavior).

The Governance Team sees the state of the entire ecosystem from a single dashboard. Compliance is not a report assembled once a quarter from self-reported spreadsheets. It is a live view: how many products are fully compliant, how many have open violations, which policies are most frequently failed, and where the trends are heading. When an auditor asks for evidence, the platform provides an immutable log showing who did what, when, and under which policy version. The forensic investigation that used to take weeks now takes minutes.

Runtime governance closes a gap that traditional approaches never solved. If a data product's quality metrics degrade beyond the threshold declared in its SLA, the platform flags it as a governance-relevant event. If freshness drifts, the marketplace updates the product's trust state. The Governance Team does not need to discover these problems by inspecting dashboards. The platform surfaces them, classifies their severity, and, if the governance rules warrant it, triggers automated workflows: notifying the team, escalating to the Domain Owner, or downgrading the product's lifecycle state until the issue is resolved.

What Success Looks Like

Delivery speeds up while risk decreases. Teams understand the rules because they are clear, consistent, and embedded in their workflow. Compliance is automatic, visible, and fair. The Governance Team spends its time designing better policies and analyzing ecosystem-wide trends, rather than chasing individual teams for evidence or running manual audits. Trust increases between governance and delivery teams, between domains, and across the organization, because rules are applied transparently, explained when they block, and evolved with care.

Data Consumer

Who They Are

The Data Consumer is any person, team, or system that uses a Data Product to answer a question, make a decision, build an analysis, or feed another process. They could be business analysts, data scientists, software engineers, decision-makers, or automated pipelines. Their work depends on getting reliable answers quickly, and on having a clear path from exploration to production use without unnecessary delays or uncertainty.

What They Care About

Data Consumers care about finding the right data quickly, using the terms and concepts they understand. They need to know exactly what the data means—not just column names or field types, but the real-world concepts, definitions, and business rules behind it, expressed in plain language and linked to the enterprise glossary or ontology. They need to know how to use the data effectively, with clear examples, sample queries, and integration guidance that lets them go from discovery to first productive use without delays.

They need to trust what they find, with clear signals about quality, reliability, and relevance. They need access without friction, through processes that respect their autonomy and time. They need to understand the impact of change before it affects their work. And they need to give and receive feedback in a way that shapes the product roadmap they depend on. In short, they want to spend their time using data to create value, not chasing approvals, reconciling conflicting sources, or guessing how to interpret or apply the dataset in practice.

Life Before the Platform

Before the enabling platform, the consumer's journey often began with uncertainty. They searched for data across multiple tools and repositories, never sure which source was authoritative. Naming conventions were inconsistent, documentation (when it existed) was scattered across wikis or hidden in personal folders, and metadata was incomplete or outdated.

Requests for access meant long email threads, unclear ownership, and sometimes manual IT tickets. The process could take days or weeks, and progress was rarely visible. Even when access was granted, the integration step was risky—the consumer often only discovered data quality issues, stale data, or unexpected schema changes once they were already deep into their work.

Change management was opaque. A schema change or contract update could break a downstream report or pipeline without warning. Feedback loops were weak or non-existent: a consumer might point out an issue, but never know whether it was fixed or even acknowledged. As a result, many consumers resorted to copying data "just in case," creating shadow datasets that drifted from the source and eroded trust.

With the Platform in Place

The Data Consumer starts in the marketplace. They do not search with technical field names or table identifiers. They type "customer revenue by country"—the business question they need to answer—and the marketplace returns results ranked by relevance to business concepts from the enterprise ontology. The search understands synonyms, domain jargon, and concept hierarchies because every data product that passed curation had its fields linked to the business glossary.

The consumer finds a product called "Customer Revenue (EU)." The product page reads like a real product page: purpose, owner, SLA commitments (freshness updated daily by 07:00 CET, 99.5% availability over rolling 30 days), quality metrics (completeness 99.8%, no nulls on revenue fields), data contract version, lineage showing the upstream sources, sample queries for the SQL and API output ports, and consumer ratings from fourteen existing users. Trust signals are prominent—not because someone wrote marketing copy, but because the curation process filled every field and the observability layer keeps the numbers current. The SLA compliance chart shows the last ninety days. Two breaches, both resolved within four hours. The consumer can make an informed decision before requesting access. The consumer clicks "Request Access" on the SQL output port. The platform routes the approval to the Data Product Owner based on the access policy configured for that product. For products classified as "open internal," approval is automatic. For products with restricted access, the owner receives a notification with the requester's identity, team, and stated purpose.

The consumer sees the request status in real time—submitted, approved, provisioning, ready—replacing the silence and uncertainty of the old process. Once approved, ACL changes are applied automatically: credentials are issued, the endpoint is exposed, and a confirmation arrives with connection instructions specific to the consumer's tooling (a JDBC string for their BI tool, an API key for their notebook). No manual IT ticket. No email to an infrastructure team. No waiting days to discover that the wrong permissions were applied.

If the product supports multiple output protocols—SQL, API, event stream, or file export—the consumer can choose the one that fits their stack directly from the marketplace, without extra meetings or custom integration work. Before wiring the product into a production dashboard, the consumer checks the observability endpoints. Yesterday's load met the contract: freshness on time, quality checks passed, no incidents. The consumer subscribes to change notifications for this product. If the producer plans a schema change, a deprecation, or a major version update, the consumer will receive the announcement through the platform before anything changes in production.

The consumer also checks the lineage graph. The product draws from three upstream sources. One of them is flagged with a recent quality warning: a completeness drop last week, now resolved. The consumer can review this history and decide whether the current state aligns with their risk tolerance. Integration becomes a deliberate step, informed by the product's operational reality, not a leap of faith.

After using the product for two weeks, the consumer leaves feedback in the marketplace: a four-star rating and a comment requesting an additional field—tax jurisdiction—that would save their team a manual enrichment step. The Data Product Owner sees the feedback alongside adoption metrics: 32 active consumers, 12 new in the last month, and an increasing average query volume. The feedback is not lost in a Slack thread or a forgotten email. It is attached to the product, visible to other consumers, and tracked as a potential enhancement in the product's roadmap. Over time, this feedback loop shapes what gets built next. Products that receive consistent feedback evolve. Products that receive none are candidates for review. The marketplace becomes a two-way channel, not a one-way catalog.

Some consumers do not stop at consumption. A data scientist who has been using the "Customer Revenue (EU)" product discovers that combining it with a marketing attribution dataset would create a high-value analytical product for the commercial team. She clicks "Build on this product" in the marketplace. The platform creates a new data product skeleton with the access agreement already in place and the lineage connection to the upstream product pre-configured. She is now a producer, and the platform supported the transition without forcing her into a separate, disjointed experience.

What Success Looks Like

The time from search to the first correct answer shrinks dramatically. Consumers stop copying data "just in case" because they trust the source—trust backed by observable SLA compliance, not by someone's verbal promise. Access is predictable, transparent, and quick. Changes are communicated before they impact production work. The marketplace becomes the front door to trusted insight. Producers and consumers engage in a healthy feedback loop, driving continuous improvement on both sides.

Key Takeaways

The Data Consumer's relationship with data is fundamentally about trust—trust that the data is what it claims to be, that access will be granted predictably, and that breaking changes will be communicated before they cause harm. A marketplace that delivers discovery in business language, automatic access fulfillment, and observable contract status converts consumers from passive recipients into active participants in the data ecosystem. With these five journeys mapped, chapter 6 turns to operational reality—how to build the platform team, drive adoption without coercion, and keep the platform healthy as the organization scales.

SIX

How To Operate the Platform

A successful Data Product Management Platform depends as much on organizational dynamics as it does on technology. The relationship between the platform team and data product teams is one of the most delicate parts of the operating model. If you get it wrong, the platform becomes a bottleneck, adoption slows down, and teams quietly work around it. If you get it right, the platform becomes a multiplier: teams move faster, governance becomes natural, and the ecosystem scales without constant coordination.

This relationship should follow a self-service model, and Team Topologies gives us a useful way to describe it. The platform team should act as an enabling platform: they build and operate a platform that product teams can consume independently. Data product teams should not depend on the platform team for day-to-day delivery, and the platform team should avoid becoming a "ticket factory" that sits in the critical path of deployments, upgrades, or operations.

Self-service does not mean "no interaction". It means structured interaction. The platform team creates capabilities, guardrails, and automation. Data product teams use them autonomously. Friction will always exist because you are coordinating work across organizational boundaries, and because standards impose constraints.

The goal is not to eliminate friction entirely, but to minimize it, keep it predictable, and ensure it is always perceived as "worth it".

When friction grows uncontrolled, the negative effects are consistent:

- Platform adoption drops, even if the platform is technically good.
- Teams revert to bespoke solutions, increasing fragmentation.
- Governance becomes bypassed or ignored because it feels hostile.
- Trust erodes and every change becomes political.

A healthy ambition looks different:

- Teams feel the platform protects them rather than policing them.
- Change feels guided rather than imposed.
- Most interactions happen through the product, not through meetings.
- The platform earns trust by reducing effort, not by requesting it.

Building the Platform Team

If there is one mistake that undermines more platform initiatives than any architectural flaw, it is treating the platform team as a project team rather than as a product team. A Data Product Management Platform is not something you "deliver" and move on from. It is a living system that evolves continuously, shaped by adoption, feedback, and organizational change. For this reason, the platform team must be designed as a long-lived product team, with its own mission, roadmap, and lifecycle, clearly decoupled from the change management of individual data products.

This distinction is not semantic; it has very concrete consequences. A project team is optimized for delivery within a fixed scope and timeframe. A product team is optimized for sustained value creation under uncertainty. A platform belongs firmly to the second category. Its success depends on resilience, continuity, and the ability to evolve without being constantly restructured or re-prioritized every time a data product team changes direction.

Following the principles described in Team Topologies, the platform team provides a service. It does not facilitate the work of data product teams, and it does not collaborate with them on delivery. This separation is essential. The moment the platform team starts embedding itself in data product initiatives, it becomes coupled to their timelines, trade-offs, and local priorities. Over time, this coupling destroys the very thing the platform is supposed to provide: a stable, predictable, and evolvable foundation.

To make this separation tangible, interactions between data product teams and the platform team should happen primarily through ticketed support. This is not about bureaucracy; it is about clarity. A ticketed model establishes explicit expectations, clear ownership, and prioritization based on platform-level value rather than local urgency. Data product teams interact with the platform as product users, not as informal collaborators negotiating bespoke solutions.

The Platform Product Manager

Because the platform is a product, it needs a product manager. This role is mandatory and cannot be treated as a secondary responsibility. Someone must be accountable for understanding user needs, prioritizing work, and connecting platform evolution to the broader objectives of the organization.

A good platform product manager spends time with users, conducting interviews with data product owners, engineers, governance teams, and consumers to understand where friction actually exists. They translate these insights into a coherent roadmap, balancing short-term adoption blockers with long-term strategic capabilities. They continuously report progress and outcomes to stakeholders, not in terms of features delivered, but in terms of problems solved and value unlocked.

At its core, product management is the discipline of connecting the company's mission with user needs, and discovering pockets of value that move both forward at the same time. In the context of a Data Product Management Platform, this means aligning platform evolution with the organization's journey towards decentralization, standardization, and scalable data management.

One of the most common and damaging errors is assigning the product manager role to the most technically powerful person in the room. The engineer who always fixes everything, who understands infrastructure automation, CI/CD, and data engineering frameworks inside out, is an invaluable asset—but they are rarely a good fit for platform product management. Their strength lies in deciding how to build something, not in deciding what should be built next or why. These profiles are far better positioned as product owners or lead engineers: people who shape technical solutions once priorities have been set, who ensure architectural coherence, and who guide implementation choices. Confusing these roles leads to platforms that are technically elegant but misaligned with real user and company needs, over-optimized for edge cases, and slow to gain adoption.

The platform product manager should still have an engineering background, enough to understand technical constraints and trade-offs, but their primary strength lies elsewhere. Very often, this role is an excellent fit for an enterprise architect: someone skilled at connecting business problems to socio-technical systems, and at moving fluently between strategy and execution. This is the essence of what Architect Elevator describes so well—

the ability to operate at multiple altitudes, from executive intent down to technical implications, without losing coherence.

Building the Technical Platform Team

Once product leadership is in place, the next step is to build the technical team that implements and maintains the platform. A platform, by its nature, spans many domains, which is reflected in the skills required. Data architecture, data engineering, AI engineering, and data analysis are all essential, particularly the ability to understand how data is actually used across the organization. Infrastructure automation, software delivery lifecycle practices, security, and governance capabilities are equally critical.

The goal is not to assemble a team of specialists working in silos, but to create a genuinely cross-functional unit. Not everyone needs to be allocated full-time to the platform, especially in the early stages, but the platform team must have regular, structured access to people with these competencies. What matters is not headcount, but critical thinking and shared ownership of the platform's evolution.

In large enterprises, once the platform has reached a certain level of maturity and adoption, the size of the platform team typically stabilizes somewhere between two or three full-time equivalents in simpler environments, and seven or eight in highly complex organizations with widespread adoption. Importantly, the size of the platform team depends on the platform's success. Growth in the team often signals increased usage, broader scope, and higher impact. While it may look like a rising cost, it is more accurately interpreted as evidence that the platform has become central to how the organization works.

Ways of Working

Because the platform team is a product team, it must adopt a way of working that supports discovery, focus, and sustainable pace. One methodology that fits particularly well in this context is Shape Up, originally developed at Basecamp. Rather than planning work through endless backlogs and short iterations, Shape Up organizes work into fixed-length cycles, with a strong emphasis on shaping problems upfront before committing to solutions.

This approach is well suited to platform work because it encourages deliberate prioritization, protects the team from constant interruptions, and creates space to address complex, cross-cutting problems without fragmenting attention. It reinforces the idea that the platform is not a reactive service desk, but a product with intentional evolution.

Support remains an essential responsibility of the platform team, but it should be delivered through a structured ticketing system. This allows the team to balance support with product development, identify recurring pain points, and feed real usage data back into the roadmap.

The Role of the Enabling Team

Alongside the platform team, it is often extremely valuable to establish an enabling team, again following Team Topologies principles. Sometimes called an adoption team, this group focuses explicitly on helping data product teams onboard, understand, and adopt the platform effectively.

This team typically combines strong knowledge of the platform with skills in data architecture and data engineering. Its goal is not to own delivery, but to accelerate learning. In some cases, the enabling team may temporarily contribute delivery capacity, working alongside data product teams in a shadowing model. This on-the-job training has a powerful effect: it demonstrates support, helps teams reach their goals within agreed timelines, and creates a flywheel effect in which early successes drive further adoption.

Crucially, the enabling team does not replace the platform team, nor does it blur boundaries. It exists to reduce friction during adoption, not to become a permanent intermediary.

Governance as Part of the Platform

Finally, there is often confusion about where data governance fits into this picture. In a mature setup, governance is not an external function policing the platform; it is an integral part of the platform team's mission. Governance expertise can be embedded directly within the platform team, or it can contribute in a more federated way, providing input and acting as a demand for the implementation of automated governance rules. What matters is that governance requirements are translated into computational policies within the platform—the same executable, deterministic checks described in chapter 4—rather than remaining as documentation or manual reviews. In this model, governance does not slow teams down; it scales with them.

Communication

The platform team must have a way to reach users, and that should be the platform itself. Communication needs to be contextual to what users are doing. If a data product team is deploying and a policy is about to become stricter, the platform should tell them at that moment, in the flow of work, with actionable language. The platform is the only channel that guarantees you are speaking to the right person at the right time, because it is where the work happens.

At the same time, platform communication cannot live only inside the platform. Attention is scarce and fragmented. People live in email, Slack, Teams, and ticketing systems. So communication should be multi-channel, but consistent: the platform remains the source of truth, while external channels amplify and ensure visibility.

Most importantly, communication must be proactive. If users discover changes by bumping into them, they will interpret the platform as unreliable and hostile. Proactive communication builds predictability, and predictability builds trust. A platform team typically needs several types of communication:

- **Broadcast communication:** Used for general announcements, including new releases, new features, upcoming improvements, and roadmap highlights. The goal is awareness, not urgency. It should be concise, regular, and consistent in structure so users learn how to scan it quickly.

- **Operational communication for incidents and disruptions:** When something breaks or service degrades, you need fast, clear communication. This is where credibility is built or destroyed. Users want to know what is affected, who is impacted, what the workaround is, and when the next update will come. Even when you don't have all the answers, a clear status update reduces anxiety and prevents chaos.

- **Planned maintenance communication:** Maintenance is acceptable when it is predictable. Users need notice, timing, expected impact, and what they should do, if anything. A good platform also makes maintenance visible where it matters: if a team is about to deploy during a maintenance window, the platform should warn them.

- **Targeted communication:** Not every message is for everyone. Some changes affect only specific domains, technologies, or types of data products. The platform

should notify only the relevant owners and consumers based on metadata, dependencies, and ownership. This is one of the strongest advantages of a data product platform: it can use the ecosystem graph to avoid noisy, irrelevant messaging.

- **Evolution communication:** This is the communication that accompanies platform evolution: changes in policies, new standards, new recommended patterns, deprecations, and capability upgrades. It must explain "why", not just "what". Users accept change when the benefit is visible and when the narrative respects their constraints.

There is a failure mode that many platform teams fall into: they communicate too much. This creates **attention overload**. When users receive too many notifications, they stop reading them. This is the classic overload effect: the signal-to-noise ratio drops, attention collapses, and the organization becomes blind exactly when you need it to be attentive. To prevent this, communication needs governance too:

- Keep broadcasts periodic rather than constant.
- Use severity levels and consistent templates.
- Prefer targeted messages over global ones.
- Make notifications actionable, not informational.
- Allow users to control what they receive, within reasonable limits.

Communication is not a courtesy.

It is part of the platform's contract with its users. When done well, it turns change into something predictable and non-threatening.

Platform Change Management

One of the most critical moments in the platform team-data product team relationship is when the platform introduces a breaking change. This is the moment where friction spikes, trust is tested, and adoption can regress. If teams experience platform evolution as disruption, they will naturally resist future changes, and eventually they will resist the platform itself.

The first rule is that breaking changes must be rare. A platform that constantly breaks its own users is not a platform; it is a moving target. Breaking changes are acceptable only when they introduce a benefit that is meaningful and perceived as such by users. The benefit cannot be a "platform team preference". It cannot be an internal refactoring disguised as progress. Users measure value in reduced effort, increased reliability, better autonomy, and lower risk.

When the benefit is real, the second rule becomes crucial: make migration as easy as possible, ideally automatic.

Human dynamics matter here. Data product teams do not experience migration work as neutral. They experience it as:

- An interruption to their roadmap.

- An unplanned cost.
- A forced reallocation of attention.
- A reminder that the platform can hurt them.

This is why migrations generate resentment when handled poorly. And resentment is not rational; it is emotional and cumulative.

Teams will remember the pain long after the technical change is done.

There is a particularly toxic pattern: when a migration is manual but users can clearly see that it could have been automated. In that situation, teams do not just feel the migration is costly; they feel it is **unfair**. They interpret it as the platform offloading work onto them. Even if the platform team did not intend that, perception becomes reality. So a strong migration approach includes:

- **Clear justification**: The "why" and the business value, not just the technical reasoning.
- **Impact visibility**: Who is affected, what needs to change, and what breaks if nothing is done.
- **Migration tooling**: Automated refactors, validators, compatibility checkers, guided scripts.
- **Compatibility windows**: Support old and new paths in parallel where possible.
- **Deprecation mechanics**: Warnings first, enforcement later, removal last.

- **Ownership clarity**: Who does what, and what the platform will do for the user.

This is also where a marketplace and dependency graph become powerful. The platform can identify downstream consumers, notify them, and coordinate change without central planning. Migration becomes a guided, observable process rather than a chaotic scramble.

A migration done well has an unexpected side effect: it increases trust. Users start to believe that the platform evolves responsibly, that change is predictable, and that the platform team respects their time.

Educate Before Enforcing

The third theme is often underestimated and yet it is decisive: educate before enforcement. Before introducing enforcement mechanisms—quality gates, computational policies, stricter checks, new mandatory metadata, or more demanding delivery rules—you must ensure users understand the value. If enforcement arrives before understanding, users will experience it as punishment. They will see governance as bureaucracy, and the platform team as gatekeepers.

This is not just a cultural issue; it becomes an adoption issue. If the platform team is perceived as a source of friction, data product teams will generate an equal and opposite reaction. They will resist, work around, delay, and in some cases actively undermine the platform by reverting to shadow practices. This resistance is not because teams hate governance. It is because they hate governance that feels arbitrary, unexplained, or imposed without empathy. A better approach is gradual:

- **Create awareness:** Explain what the rule protects, and what risks it prevents. Use concrete examples such as downstream breakages, audit failures, security incidents, operational disruptions. People adopt rules when they connect them to real pain they recognize.
- **Provide guidance and good defaults:** If you want teams to do the right thing, make the right thing the easiest thing. Templates, descriptors, golden paths, and examples reduce cognitive load. They also reduce interpretation variance, which is often the hidden source of governance failure.
- **Introduce a grace period:** A grace period is not a compromise; it is part of the adoption strategy. During this period, policies run in warning mode. Teams can see what would fail, learn what to fix, and plan changes without blocking delivery. The platform builds habits before it builds enforcement.
- **Enforce when readiness is high:** Enforcement should occur when most teams are already compliant and non-compliance is the exception rather than the norm. At that point, enforcement feels like consistency, not oppression.

This approach aligns with DevOps thinking: shift left, provide fast feedback, reduce surprises, and make quality objective. Enforcement becomes a stabilizer, not a barrier.

Minimizing friction between platform teams and data product teams is not a soft concern. It determines whether the platform will scale or stall:

- A healthy platform–product relationship is **self-service by design**, not collaboration by necessity.
- **Communication** must be proactive, contextual, multi-channel, and carefully controlled to avoid attention overload.
- **Migration paths** must be rare, justified, and as automated as possible, because migrations test trust more than anything else.

Enablement and autonomy are not abstract ideals; they are concrete outcomes of deliberate platform design. Teams do not become autonomous because we tell them they are. They become autonomous when the platform removes friction, reduces cognitive load, and gives them safe freedom to act without constant coordination.

In a Data Product Management Platform, autonomy does **not** mean lack of constraints. Quite the opposite. Autonomy scales only when constraints are explicit, well-designed, and enforced consistently. The role of the platform team is therefore not to control teams, but to **shape the environment** in which teams operate so that doing the right thing is easy, and doing the wrong thing is hard.

This chapter explores the mechanisms that maximize enablement while preserving safety: guardrails, templates and blueprints, eliminating tickets, automation as a first-class concern, and a user experience that supports multiple skill levels without fragmenting the platform.

Guardrails

The concept of **guardrails** is central to enablement. Guardrails are constraints that guide behavior without prescribing every step. They define the safe operating boundaries within which teams are free to move.

Rules tend to be static, verbose, and externally imposed. Guardrails are embedded, executable, and contextual. A rule says "you must do X". A guardrail makes it impossible, or at least very hard, to do anything else. Good guardrails share a few properties:

- They are encoded in the platform, not documented in slides.
- They are enforced automatically, not manually.
- They explain *why* when they block an action.
- They leave room for variation and evolution.

Guardrails are what allow autonomy to exist without turning into chaos.

Templates: Solving the Blank Page Problem (and Their Risks)

One of the biggest enemies of autonomy is the **blank page syndrome**. When teams are given unlimited freedom and no starting point, delivery slows, decisions multiply, and inconsistency explodes. Templates are the first and most effective antidote to this problem.

Templates provide a concrete starting point. They encode conventions, defaults, and best practices so teams do not have to reinvent them every time. This is particularly important in data products, where descriptors often take the form of YAML or similar configuration files.

However, templates also come with risks. YAML, while flexible, is unforgiving. Small syntax errors cause failures that are hard to debug. Large YAML files quickly become opaque, especially for less technical users. When templates become too complex, teams stop understanding what they are editing and start blindly copying and pasting. At that point, templates no longer enable; they obscure. For templates to be effective:

- They must be minimal, not exhaustive.
- They must contain sensible defaults, not placeholders everywhere.
- They must be documented *inline*, not externally.

- They must evolve carefully to avoid breaking existing usage.

Templates should reduce decision-making, not merely shift it into configuration.

Blueprints: From Starting Points to Intentional Design

Where templates provide a starting point, **blueprints** provide structure.

A blueprint defines *what a data product is composed of and how its components relate to one another.* It captures architectural intent rather than implementation detail. Blueprints make explicit the composition of a data product: storage layers, processing components, output ports, policies, and operational characteristics.

Blueprints matter because they allow the platform to reason about data products at a higher level of abstraction. They enable:

- Dependency-aware orchestration.
- Consistent deployment strategies.
- Predictable operational behavior.
- Meaningful governance checks.

Unlike templates, blueprints are not edited frequently by teams. They are usually selected or parameterized. This distinction is important. Templates are tactical. Blueprints are strategic.

A platform that offers a small, well-curated set of blueprints enables diversity without fragmentation. Teams can choose the blueprint that fits their use case, while the platform retains the ability to automate, govern, and support the product effectively.

Templates vs Frameworks

We have already discussed at length why frameworks are a dangerous choice for platform enablement. The short version: frameworks create coupling, introduce systemic risk through shared dependencies, and inevitably become obstacles when use cases outgrow their original design. Templates avoid all of this. They provide a starting point without introducing runtime dependencies, and teams own the code from the moment of creation. If teams need to understand the internals of the platform to be productive, the platform has failed its enablement mission.

Zero Tickets Goal

Nothing kills autonomy faster than tickets.

Tickets introduce waiting time, ambiguity, and hidden prioritization. They reintroduce a client–supplier dynamic that platforms are explicitly meant to remove. When teams need to open a ticket to deploy, gain access, or fix an operational issue, the platform becomes a bottleneck by definition.

A self-service platform should aim for ***zero tickets in the happy path****.*

This does not mean that support disappears. It means that support is reserved for exceptional cases, not routine operations. Deployments, upgrades, access requests, rollbacks, and validations must all be executable directly by teams through the platform.

When tickets exist:

- Teams batch requests to reduce friction.
- Work slows down artificially.
- Urgency is lost in prioritization queues.
- Ownership becomes blurred.

Removing tickets forces the platform team to invest in automation, documentation, and UX. This is a good thing. Every ticket avoided is a signal that the platform has become more mature.

Enablement does not scale through process; it scales through automation.

Automation is not about saving time in isolation. It is about removing coordination costs. Every manual step is a place where autonomy breaks down and dependencies reappear.

In a Data Product Management Platform, automation must cover:

- Provisioning and deprovisioning.
- Deployment and undeployment.
- Policy enforcement.
- Metadata publication.
- Access granting.
- Validation and auditing.

Automation must also be **deterministic**. Teams should be able to reliably predict outcomes. If the same input sometimes succeeds and sometimes fails, autonomy collapses because teams no longer trust the platform.

Importantly, automation must be visible. Black-box automation increases anxiety. Teams need to see what is happening, what failed, and what to do next. Good automation always comes with good observability.

Finally, autonomy depends on user experience—and not just for one type of user.

A Data Product Management Platform is used by people with very different skills:

- Data engineers.
- Analytics engineers.
- Data scientists.
- Platform engineers.
- Business users.
- Governance and compliance roles.

Designing separate tools for each persona fragments the ecosystem and increases integration cost. The alternative is a **multi-skill UX**: one platform, one model, multiple entry points. A multi-skill UX:

- Adapts language and defaults to the user's context.
- Exposes complexity progressively.
- Prioritizes business concepts over technical ones when appropriate.
- Does not hide power from expert users.

This does not mean building multiple UIs for each role. It means building a coherent experience that can be navigated at different depths. The same data product can be explored at a business level or inspected at a technical level without switching tools.

When UX fails to accommodate different skill levels, teams compensate by creating side channels, shadow documentation, and bespoke workflows. Autonomy erodes silently.

Platform ROI

One of the most underestimated challenges in building and operating a platform is not technical complexity, adoption, or governance. It is justification.

The fact that an organization has, at some point, endorsed the creation of a Data Product Management Platform does not mean the discussion is closed forever. Management changes. Strategic priorities shift. Economic pressure fluctuates. New technologies appear and old ones fall out of fashion. At any moment, from almost any corner of the organization, someone may ask a very simple question: *Why are we still investing in this platform?*

The challenge may come from finance, a business domain, an antagonistic working group, or a new executive who was not present when the original decision was made. This is why platform ROI cannot be treated as a one-off business case created to unlock initial funding. It must be a continuous practice.

From the very beginning, it is essential to define a method to calculate the return on investment of the platform, to compute it proactively, and to communicate it as soon as meaningful results start to emerge. Waiting until the platform is questioned puts the team in a defensive position, where every number feels like a justification rather than an observation.

Why Platform ROI is a Difficult Topic

Calculating the ROI of a platform is inherently difficult because a platform is primarily an enabler of a new way of working. It does not generate direct revenue. In most cases, it does not even have cost savings as its primary objective. Its real value lies in enabling decentralization, improving consistency, reducing friction, and allowing data products to scale without collapsing under their own complexity.

As a consequence, the return on investment is largely indirect. It emerges through second-order effects, making framing and narrative just as important as the numbers themselves. A good ROI model for a platform does not try to "prove" that the platform makes money. Instead, it shows how the organization would spend *more* money, time, and energy without it.

To make this tangible, it is useful to distinguish between two broad categories of ROI drivers.

The first category includes what we can call *soft returns*: improvements in user experience, reduced cognitive load, greater adoption of data products, better data quality, and clearer ownership. These aspects are real and impactful, but hard to monetize directly.

The second category includes *hard returns*: measurable reductions in effort, lead time, defects, duplicated work, operational overhead, and governance cost. These are the dimensions where a quantitative model can and should be built.

A solid ROI narrative needs both. Soft returns explain *why* the platform matters. Hard returns explain *why it is economically rational.*

A Practical Model for Platform ROI

Over time, a fairly standard pattern emerges when organizations start measuring the impact of a Data Product Management

Platform. While numbers will vary, the underlying structure is surprisingly consistent.

Operational and Deployment Efficiency

One of the first and most visible sources of ROI comes from standardization and automation in deployment and operations.

Before the platform, preparing a new solution or a new data product typically involved a long chain of tickets, manual reviews, infrastructure setup, and coordination across multiple teams. Each step may seem reasonable in isolation, but together they create significant friction.

With the platform in place, much of this effort is absorbed by templates, automated governance checks, and repeatable deployment patterns. The savings do not come from doing *less work*, but from doing the same work once and reusing it many times. This shows up in several ways:

- Fewer days spent preparing a new domain.
- Fewer days required to bootstrap a new data product.
- Faster and more predictable deployments.
- Reduced operational effort for recurring deployments.

When multiplied by the number of data products and by the number of deployments per year, these small efficiencies accumulate into substantial savings.

Reduction of Support Load and Tickets

Another tangible effect is the reduction in support tickets directed to platform, infrastructure, and operations teams.

A self-service platform with clear boundaries, standardized interfaces, and automated checks naturally reduces the need for human intervention. Teams do not open fewer tickets because they are discouraged, but because many problems simply no longer exist.

Even a modest reduction in ticket volume, combined with a conservative estimate of the effort required to handle each ticket, results in a measurable saving over time. This effect is particularly important because support effort scales poorly with adoption. Without a platform, every new data product increases the load on central teams.

Governance Efficiency

Governance is often perceived as a pure cost center, but in reality, it is an area where platforms can achieve significant efficiency gains.

Without a platform, governance teams spend a significant amount of time manually reviewing artifacts, checking compliance, managing exceptions, and supporting audits. With a Data Product Management Platform, a large portion of this work moves from manual control to automated enforcement.

This translates into:

- Fewer days spent by governance teams on each new data product.
- Lower effort to manage evolutions and breaking changes.
- Reduced audit preparation time thanks to standardized tracking and auditability.

These savings grow over time as the number of data products increases, because automated governance scales linearly while manual governance does not scale at all.

Defect Reduction and Quality Effects

Quality improvements are often categorized as "soft", but they have very concrete economic consequences.

A platform that enforces standard patterns, validates changes upfront, and embeds quality checks into the lifecycle reduces the number of defects that reach production. Each avoided defect saves time on investigation, rework, coordination, and often reputational damage across teams.

Even with conservative assumptions, reducing the number of defects and the effort required to fix them yields a steady, recurring saving.

Project Management and Discovery Efficiency

An often-overlooked dimension of ROI is the efficiency gains in discovery and project management.

A clear marketplace, explicit ownership, and visible existing data products reduce duplicated analysis, unnecessary initiatives, and wasted alignment effort. Teams spend less time figuring out *what exists* and *who owns it*, and more time actually building value.

This shows up as a reduction in effort during the early phases of initiatives, particularly in large organizations where a lack of visibility is a major source of inefficiency.

What Is Often Missing from ROI Models

Many ROI models stop here, but there are additional dimensions worth considering.

One is data duplication. Even if not immediately reduced, the platform creates the conditions to *observe* duplication and act on it deliberately rather than accidentally.

Another is risk reduction. Faster audits, better traceability, and clearer ownership reduce regulatory and operational risk. While difficult to monetize, this dimension is often highly valued by senior management.

Finally, there is opportunity cost. Faster lead times and greater confidence in data products enable the organization to pursue opportunities it would otherwise avoid. This is rarely captured in spreadsheets, but it is very real.

Communicating Platform ROI Without Being Defensive

Calculating ROI is only half of the job. How it is communicated matters just as much.

A common mistake is to treat ROI communication as a defensive exercise, triggered only when the platform is questioned. This usually leads to pushy presentations, overloaded spreadsheets, and a narrative that feels like justification rather than insight.

A more effective approach is to communicate ROI proactively, lightly, and continuously.

One practical pattern is to embed ROI signals into existing governance and reporting rhythms. Instead of creating a dedicated "ROI presentation", the platform team periodically shares a short update that highlights concrete outcomes: time saved, tickets avoided, audits simplified, and adoption growth. These updates should be factual, not celebratory.

Another effective technique is to anchor ROI communication to real stories. Rather than leading with numbers, start with a concrete before-and-after scenario, then connect it to measurable effects. This keeps the conversation grounded and avoids abstract claims.

Finally, it is important to tailor the message to the audience. Finance cares about cost and predictability. Domain leaders care about speed and autonomy. Governance cares about control and risk. The same underlying ROI model can support all these narratives, but the framing must change.

The goal is not to prove that the platform is indispensable. It is to make its impact visible enough that questioning its value feels artificial.

Key Takeaways

- Platform ROI cannot be a one-off business case. It must be measured continuously and communicated proactively.
- Soft returns (experience, quality, ownership clarity) explain why the platform matters. Hard returns (effort, lead time, defects, governance cost) explain why it is economically rational.
- The strongest ROI argument is not "look how much we saved" but "look how much more the organization would spend without it."
- Communicate ROI through facts and stories, not through defensive presentations. Tailor the message to the audience.

Chapter 7 examines what follows successful adoption—how organizations mature with their platforms, how the model evolves as AI enters the picture, and what the long-term trajectory of the platformization journey looks like.

SEVEN

Maturity, Evolution, and What Comes Next

Platformization is often framed as an advanced stage of organizational evolution. Many enterprises treat it as a destination reserved for companies that have already achieved high maturity in governance, data management, and automation. This assumption is not only misleading; it is actively harmful.

Waiting for maturity before investing in a data product management platform creates a paradox. Maturity does not emerge in isolation, through policies, frameworks, or conceptual alignment alone. It grows through practice, friction, experimentation, and feedback. Organizations become mature by operating systems that force them to confront ownership, quality, change management, and accountability in concrete, day-to-day decisions. In this sense, platformization is not the reward for maturity. It is one of its strongest accelerators.

A data product management platform should not be perceived as a heavy, opinionated structure imposed on teams. When designed correctly, it becomes a progressive enabler: a system that grows with the organization, increases awareness first, then automation, and finally enforcement, without ever becoming a bottleneck. The platform evolves alongside the organization, shaping behaviors as it absorbs complexity.

This chapter explores platformization as a gradual journey. It explains how data product management platforms can drive organizational maturity, unlock AI at scale, and naturally converge on a data fabric model in which data, semantics, and AI agents operate as a coherent system.

This final part of the book examines the relationship between platform adoption and organizational maturity across three chapters. The first shows why the platform, by making inconsistencies unavoidable and questions inescapable, accelerates learning faster than any cultural initiative could alone. The second traces the three-stage adoption path—from awareness through governed automation to ecosystem-wide enforcement—and explains why governance must grow in parallel with adoption rather than ahead of it. The third examines the most consequential challenge now facing data-intensive organizations: ambiguity, and why unresolved semantic inconsistency is the true enemy of AI at scale.

This part closes the book's argument: the platform begins as an infrastructure investment and ends as an enterprise capability—the operating system for data, governance, and eventually AI-assisted decision-making.

Platformization as a Maturity Accelerator

The belief that platformization requires maturity usually stems from fear. Fear of disruption, fear of slowing down delivery, fear of exposing weaknesses in governance and data practices. These fears are understandable, but they miss a fundamental point:

Maturity is not a prerequisite for structure;
structure is what enables maturity.

The Maturity Paradox

Without a platform, governance remains aspirational. Ownership is discussed but rarely enforced. Quality is measured after the fact. Change management relies on tribal knowledge and goodwill. In this environment, every new initiative increases entropy. AI, in particular, amplifies this chaos by consuming data faster than organizations can understand or control it.

The paradox is straightforward. Organizations postpone platformization because they feel unprepared. But the things that would make them prepared—clear ownership, consistent semantics, enforceable contracts, reliable change management—are precisely the behaviors that a platform forces into existence. Waiting for maturity without introducing the structure that produces it is like waiting to be fit before starting to exercise.

How the Platform Forces Clarity

A data product management platform introduces just enough structure to make problems visible. It forces questions that were previously postponed: Who owns this data? What does this field actually mean? What happens if we change it? Who depends on it?

These questions are not new. Every organization has them. The difference is that without a platform, they remain buried in Slack threads, meeting notes, and undocumented assumptions. With a platform, they surface at the moment they matter most—when someone tries to build, deploy, or consume a data product.

Consider what happens when a team registers its first data product. The platform asks them to declare ownership, describe business meaning, and commit to a contract. Suddenly, a team that has been producing data for years discovers it cannot answer basic questions about its own output. Who is the business owner? What does the field `status` represent? Which downstream consumers depend on the current schema? The exercise itself generates more clarity in a week than months of governance workshops.

This effect compounds. Once one team's data product is visible and well described, neighboring teams face the same questions. Duplication becomes apparent. Conflicting definitions surface. The organization's real state of maturity is no longer hidden behind slide decks and maturity assessment scores—it is visible in the platform, in the gaps between what teams declared and what they actually deliver.

Acceleration Through Feedback Loops

The platform creates feedback loops that compress the distance between discovering a problem and resolving it. In a traditional governance model, an inconsistency in field semantics might take months to reach the right committee, be prioritized, and eventually result in a decision. In a platform-driven model, the inconsistency is surfaced when a consumer searches the marketplace and finds three data products claiming to represent customer revenue, each with different definitions and numbers.

That visibility creates urgency. Domain owners are confronted with evidence of overlap. Consumer complaints are traceable. The platform does not resolve the ambiguity itself, but it ensures ambiguity cannot persist invisibly.

The same dynamic applies to quality. When quality rules are embedded in contracts, failures are immediate and attributable. There is no lag between a broken promise and its detection. Teams learn faster because consequences arrive faster. Over time, the quality of data products improves not because someone mandated it from above, but because the platform made poor quality expensive to ignore.

Progressive, Not Prescriptive

The key is not to introduce everything at once. A platform that comes with 100 mandatory fields, strict deployment gates, and a long certification process will generate the same resistance as any top-down governance program. Adoption must be progressive. Start with what hurts most, usually ownership and contracts, and let the platform's own evidence guide what to enforce next.

> *Governance automation follows organizational readiness, not the other way around.*

This is the principle that separates platformization as an accelerator from platformization as a burden. The platform should make the right thing easier than the wrong thing. When it does, teams adopt it not because they are forced to, but because it removes the friction they were already experiencing.

Progressive Adoption and Progressive Governance

One of the most common failure modes of platform initiatives is over-enforcement too early. When governance automation is introduced as a rigid gate, teams perceive the platform as an obstacle rather than an enabler. Delivery slows down, workarounds proliferate, and trust erodes.

A successful platform follows a different path. It grows its enforcement capabilities in parallel with organizational awareness. Early stages focus on enablement and visibility. Only later does enforcement become stronger, and even then, it evolves incrementally. This progressive approach ensures business continuity. Processes are not broken overnight. Instead, teams gradually internalize new practices, supported by automation rather than constrained by it.

At every stage, the platform must answer a simple question: Does this capability help teams do the right thing more easily than the wrong thing?

Stage One: Awareness as the Foundation

The first stage of a data product management platform is not infrastructure automation. It is awareness. The goal is to expose why certain principles matter, without radically changing how teams build and run their systems. The platform provides lightweight automation and enablement around a small number of high-impact concepts.

Among these, data contracts represent a particularly effective starting point. Introducing data contracts early creates immediate value with minimal disruption. A data contract makes explicit what was previously implicit: the structure, meaning, and expected behavior of data exposed by a data product. More importantly, it clarifies accountability. When a team declares a data contract, it implicitly accepts responsibility for keeping it valid over time. Change management stops being an informal negotiation and becomes a visible commitment. Breaking changes are no longer accidental; they are deliberate decisions with consequences.

This shift has a profound cultural impact. Ownership stops being a label and becomes an operational reality. At the same time, data contracts reinforce data quality. Quality rules stop being generic checks applied downstream and become part of the producer's responsibility. The organization begins to internalize a simple but powerful idea: quality is not something you inspect later; it is something you promise upfront.

Crucially, this stage does not require heavy infrastructure automation. Data products continue to run on existing platforms. Teams are not forced to adopt new deployment models or operational patterns. The intervention is deliberately non-invasive. Yet, despite its light footprint, this phase dramatically increases awareness. Ambiguities become visible. Inconsistencies surface. Conversations change. People start asking better questions. This is the moment when the organization begins to understand why governance matters.

Stage Two: Governing Data Products as Atomic Units

Once awareness is established, the platform can evolve towards deeper automation, particularly around infrastructure and operations. In this second stage, data products start being treated as atomic units. Deployment, runtime operations, and lifecycle management become self-service capabilities exposed by the platform. Teams gain autonomy without compromising governance. On the contrary, governance becomes stronger precisely because it is automated.

Infrastructure compliance rules, architectural standards, security controls, and metadata requirements are embedded into the deployment process. Teams do not need to remember them; the platform enforces them by design. This shifts governance from review-based processes to executable guarantees.

Change management also matures. Because data products are managed as cohesive units, changes to schemas, contracts, or infrastructure are evaluated in context. Dependencies are explicit. Impact analysis becomes possible. Breaking changes can be managed deliberately rather than discovered accidentally.

Importantly, this stage does not reduce speed. It increases it. By removing manual approvals and replacing them with automated checks, teams move faster with more confidence. The platform absorbs complexity that would otherwise slow them down. Governance stops being a negotiation and becomes an integrated part of delivery.

This is also the stage where metadata quality improves significantly. Technical, operational, and business metadata are produced as part of normal workflows. Documentation stops being a separate activity and becomes a by-product of delivery.

Stage Three: Expanding Across the Data Landscape

The third stage extends these principles beyond traditional analytical data products. Machine learning, AI initiatives, business intelligence, and decision services are brought under the same governance and automation umbrella.

This expansion is essential. Fragmented governance across different data initiatives recreates silos and undermines trust. AI models trained on poorly governed data are unreliable by design. By applying the same data product principles across the entire data landscape, the organization creates consistency. Ownership models align. Change management becomes predictable. Automation scales.

At this stage, decentralization, self-service, and automated governance become pervasive rather than exceptional. The platform evolves from a data initiative into an enterprise capability. Policy enforcement also becomes progressively stronger. Early warnings evolve into blocking controls. Runtime policies complement deployment checks. Enforcement increases without creating discontinuities, because awareness and practices have already matured. Governance grows linearly with adoption, not in sudden jumps.

Declarative Patterns and Metadata Activation

A critical outcome of progressive adoption is the shift towards declarative patterns. Initially, declarations focus on data contracts: schemas first, then business metadata, then quality expectations. Over time, declarations expand to cover entire data products, including infrastructure, interfaces, and operational behaviors. Eventually, this declarative approach extends to all data initiatives.

This evolution naturally leads to metadata activation. Metadata stops being passive documentation and becomes an executable input for automation, governance, and reasoning. In this context, metadata quality becomes critical. Both technical and business metadata must be accurate, complete, and aligned. Poor metadata does not merely reduce discoverability; it actively blocks automation and AI.

This is where the connection with data fabric becomes evident.

Ambiguity as the Real Enemy of AI

AI systems do not fail primarily because of a lack of data, nor because models are not powerful enough. They fail because they are asked to reason in the face of ambiguity.

Ambiguity is the real systemic enemy of AI, and it lives in unmanaged data, fragmented semantics, and implicit assumptions that humans resolve informally but machines cannot.

The Ambiguity Problem

Consider a seemingly trivial request: "Give me revenues by country." For a human analyst embedded in a specific business context, this question might appear straightforward. For an AI system, it is anything but.

Which definition of revenue should be used? Gross or net? Recognized or billed? Including discounts or excluding them? At which point in time should revenue be attributed? Order date, invoice date, shipment date, or payment date? And what does "country" mean? Customer legal entity country? Shipping country? Billing country? Sales organization country? If multiple of these exist in the data landscape, which one carries business authority?

In most enterprises, all these interpretations coexist. They are encoded across different datasets, dashboards, pipelines, and reports, often created at different times by different teams for different purposes. Humans navigate this ambiguity through context, experience, and informal knowledge. AI cannot.

When an AI system is exposed to multiple tables containing a "country" field, each one technically correct but semantically different, it has no reliable way to infer which one represents the business concept behind the question. The result is uncertainty, hallucination, or overly cautious answers that provide little value. AI activation stalls at scale for precisely this reason: the data exists but remains unintelligible.

Why Enterprises Stay Stuck

The typical data problems blocking AI activation are remarkably consistent across industries. Enterprises accumulate too many similar data assets that represent the same concept at different stages of maturity or owned by different teams. Documentation is partial or outdated. Examples, formulas, and usage patterns are missing. Semantic links between datasets and business concepts are weak or entirely absent.

From an AI perspective, this environment is hostile. Every additional dataset increases the search space. Every undocumented transformation introduces uncertainty. Every missing semantic link multiplies ambiguity.

A progressive data product management platform systematically tackles this problem. By enforcing ownership, every data asset exposed through a data product has someone accountable for its meaning and behavior. By embedding data contracts, expectations become explicit and machine-readable. By progressively enriching business metadata, concepts are anchored to shared definitions. This does not eliminate ambiguity overnight. But it reduces it incrementally, in a controlled and observable way. Each data product that becomes well-defined reduces the cognitive and computational load required to reason across the landscape.

AI does not need perfect data. It needs data that is understandable.

From Data Products to a Knowledge Layer

As organizations reduce ambiguity and improve metadata quality, a natural question emerges: Is governing data products enough to unlock AI at scale? The answer is no.

Data products are a necessary foundation, but they are not sufficient on their own. To move from reliable data to actionable knowledge, enterprises must introduce an additional layer that captures meaning, relationships, and intent in a form that machines can reason over.

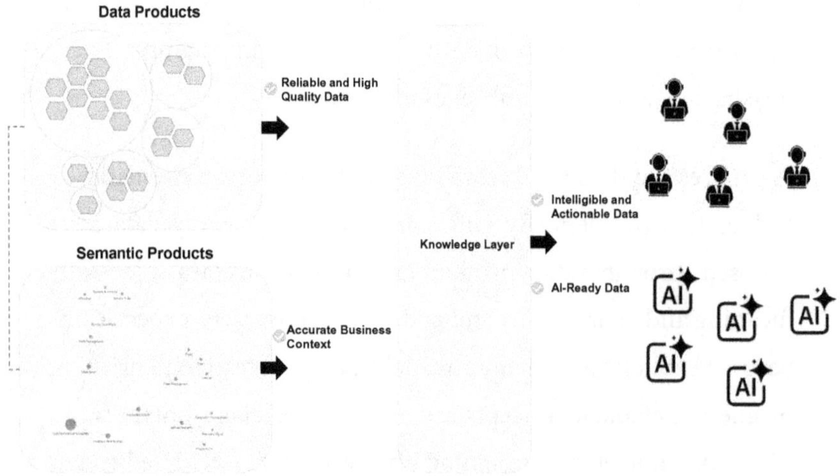

A knowledge layer emerges from combining governed data products with explicit semantic models that describe how business concepts relate to each other. Semantic products play a key role in this transition. They represent business concepts, relationships, and rules independently of physical data structures. They define what a "customer", an "order", a "contract", or a "revenue stream" means in business terms, and how these concepts connect across domains.

When semantic products are linked with data products, the organization moves beyond data availability towards data understanding. Data stops being a collection of fields and tables and becomes part of a coherent conceptual model. This blending is fundamental for AI readiness. AI systems reason over relationships, not just values. Without explicit semantics, reasoning remains shallow and brittle.

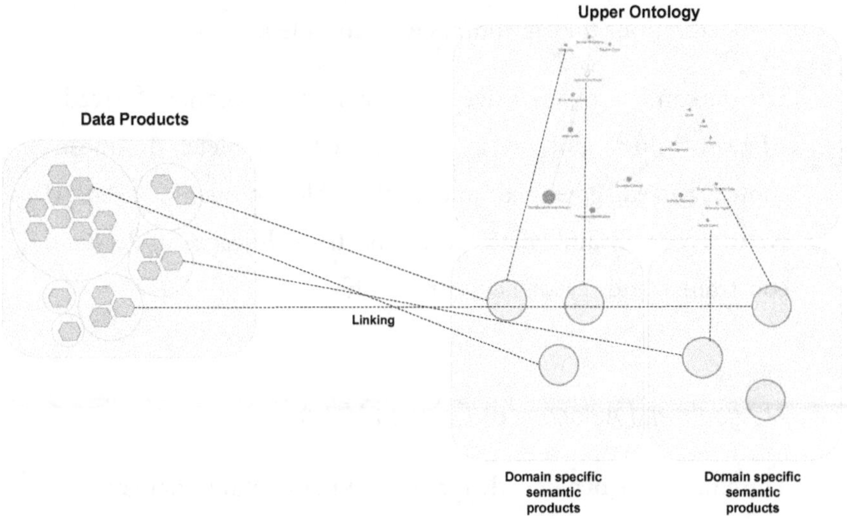

Three additional capabilities become essential at this stage:

- **Knowledge management.** The platform must capture, version, and govern business knowledge explicitly. This includes definitions, rules, assumptions, and mappings between technical representations and business concepts. Knowledge cannot remain implicit or scattered across documents and presentations.
- **Data interoperability.** Data products must expose interfaces that allow them to be combined consistently across domains. Interoperability is not only a technical concern; it is a semantic one. Two datasets are interoperable only if their concepts align.
- **Semantic-to-data linkage.** Linking semantic products to data products creates a navigable graph of meaning, where AI systems and humans can traverse from business questions to data sources with confidence.

The outcome is a knowledge layer where data becomes AI-ready. AI-ready does not mean perfect or complete. It means contextualized, governed, and explainable. In such a layer, AI systems can disambiguate concepts, trace lineage, understand constraints, and reason about trade-offs.

AI Agents and Autonomous Decision Making

The emergence of a knowledge layer fundamentally changes what is possible with AI. Most current AI initiatives stop at augmentation: assisting humans by generating summaries, answering questions, or suggesting actions. True autonomy remains limited, not because models are incapable, but because the environment they operate in is unreliable.

Autonomous AI agents require more than access to data. They require trust. Trust, in this context, is not an emotional attribute. It is a structural property of the system. An AI agent must be able to rely on the consistency of data products, the stability of semantics, and the predictability of change management processes.

When data products, semantic products, and governance mechanisms are aligned, AI agents can operate with a higher degree of independence. They can evaluate alternatives, simulate outcomes, and make decisions within defined boundaries. This autonomy is only safe if governance is embedded by design. Policies must not be external constraints applied after the fact. They must be executable rules that shape what agents can see, do, and change.

In this model, AI agents become first-class products. They have lifecycles, owners, contracts, and compliance requirements, just like data products. They consume data products, rely on semantic products, and produce decisions or actions. Managing AI agents using the same platform principles ensures coherence. Declarative definitions, progressive enforcement, and strong metadata integration apply equally to data, semantics, and AI.

Platformization as the Enterprise Operating System

This convergence reveals something larger. What started as an initiative to improve ownership, quality, and governance of data assets has evolved into a broader platformization effort encompassing data, semantics, and AI. The same principles apply across all layers: definitions are declarative rather than procedural, governance is embedded rather than enforced externally, self-service is enabled without sacrificing control, and adoption and enforcement remain progressive.

Instead of building separate platforms for data governance, knowledge management, and AI operations, enterprises can converge on a single platform foundation. Such a platform does not dictate architectures or technologies. It defines how products are described, governed, evolved, and trusted across the organization.

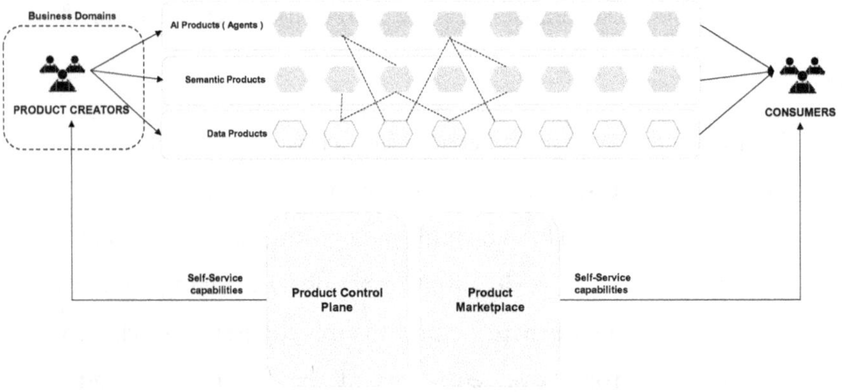

In this sense, platformization becomes the organizational substrate on which data fabrics, knowledge layers, and AI systems can emerge organically. Data fabric is not something you install. It is something that emerges when declarative data products, activated metadata, and semantic alignment reach critical mass. AI readiness is not declared; it is observed in the system's ability to support autonomous reasoning without constant human correction.

The real risk today is not investing too early in platformization.
The real risk is postponing it,
allowing ambiguity to compound while AI accelerates the consequences of every unresolved inconsistency.

In an enterprise that wants AI to move from experimentation to decision making, that operating system is no longer optional.

The conclusion that follows gathers these threads and addresses the one question every platform builder eventually faces: when has the platform done its job?

Key Takeaways

Platformization is not a final step; it is the engine of maturity. Progressive adoption, starting with awareness and evolving towards automation and enforcement, allows organizations to scale without disruption. Data products provide the foundation for intelligibility, governance, and trust. By extending these principles to semantics and AI, enterprises can build a knowledge layer that unlocks autonomous decision making. In this journey, maturity is not something you wait for. It is something you build by doing.

Conclusion

The platform is no longer a project. It has a roadmap, a team, internal users who file feature requests, and domain owners who complain when a deployment policy changes without notice. It is, by every practical measure, a product. The fact that it reached this state is not remarkable in itself. What is remarkable is how different the organization looks compared to when the journey started—and how little of that change was planned upfront.

This book makes a single, sustained argument: that a data product management platform is the operating model through which decentralized data organizations actually operate. It defines how data products are created, evolve, governed, and consumed. It is where data, knowledge, and AI converge into a single system that is both flexible and controlled—a system where autonomy does not mean chaos, and governance does not mean friction.

The platform plays a dual role. It enables teams by reducing cognitive load, guiding them through complex processes, and making self-service practical. At the same time, it enforces standards, policies, and controls consistently and at scale. Enablement and enforcement are not in conflict. They are two sides of the same mechanism.

The real shift is organizational. When the platform works as intended, it aligns people, processes, and technology around a shared way of building and managing data products. It creates a common language, a common lifecycle, and a common understanding of what good looks like. That alignment is what allows organizations to absorb the increasing role of AI in decision-making and operations—not by predicting what AI will require, but by building the semantic and governance foundations that any reliable AI system demands.

This alignment does not arrive fully formed. It follows a progression: awareness first, then automation, then enforcement. Organizations that respect this sequence build durable platforms. Those that skip ahead—enforcing policies before teams understand why they exist—produce resistance, workarounds, and eventual abandonment.

The concern we raised at the outset of this book—that decentralization without structure becomes a boomerang, eventually forcing organizations back towards the centralization they were trying to escape—finds its answer in the platform. When governance is embedded rather than imposed, when lifecycle is orchestrated rather than improvised, and when standards are encoded rather than documented, decentralization stops being a risk and becomes a sustainable operating model.

The platform absorbs complexity, structures it, and makes it usable. That is how the boomerang stays thrown.

About the Author

Paolo Platter is an entrepreneur, architect, and strategic advisor in the field of data management and platform engineering.

Over the past fifteen years, he has worked at the intersection of architecture, governance, and organizational design, helping large enterprises across multiple industries and European countries rethink how they build, manage, and scale their data ecosystems. His work has taken him inside complex organizations navigating regulatory pressure, decentralization, cloud transformation, and AI adoption—environments where data is both a strategic asset and a structural risk.

As co-founder and technical leader of Agile Lab, Paolo helped grow the company from two people with an idea into an international organization serving some of Europe's largest enterprises. Along this journey, he has been deeply involved in the architectural design of large-scale data platforms, Data Mesh initiatives, and data product operating models. But more importantly, he has observed—from the inside—how these ideas behave when confronted with real-world enterprise constraints.

Paolo has had the opportunity to observe how data practices have evolved over time—from centralized data warehouses to data lakes, from platform-centric approaches to domain-oriented models, from manual governance to computational enforcement.

He has seen what scales, what collapses, and what quietly accumulates debt until it becomes unmanageable.

His focus has always been architectural in the broadest sense: not only how systems are built, but how responsibilities are distributed, how lifecycle is enforced, how change is governed, and how autonomy can coexist with control.

Index